THE MONARCH OF TALL PINES POOL

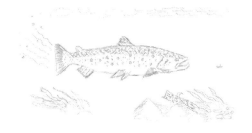

BY

RICK CRECRAFT

The Monarch of Tall Pines Pool

by Rick Crecraft

Copyright © 2017 Rick Crecraft

Published by Barefoot Publishing

All rights reserved.

Illustrated by the author

WHAT READERS ARE SAYING

"Lefty" Kreh, world-renowned fishing expert, author, and teacher, writes:

Most fishing books today are oriented toward how, when, where, and what to use to catch fish. There's nothing wrong with that, and it has helped me pay bills for most of my life. Rick Crecraft's *The Monarch of Tall Pines Pool* is different. This is a book that certainly has some how-to technique within its pages. But this is much more than that. This is a charming story almost any fisherman will enjoy. It's well told, full of suspense, and is the stuff that a fisherman's dreams are made of. This book doesn't need an index. You'll not be searching for the name of a fly pattern or special gear. This is a fun book, and I urge you to find a quiet place, a comfortable chair, and then sit back and enjoy Rick's work.

Lefty Kreh

I think you've got a great story here. The characters are both believable and likable. The reader is immersed in a world of natural beauty—which you describe beautifully. I was able to lose myself in this world and, for the time I was in it, able to escape the hustle and bustle of my complex life. The reader learns fascinating aspects of nature, things most people wouldn't know. It is a story that imparts valuable lessons on life, lessons that both young and old would do well to pay attention to.

David O'Brien

Congratulations on your book! I spent every summer in Maine as a boy, and I relate to all the experiences so well portrayed in your book. You show a great appreciation of nature and the physical sciences. Having finished your book, I am ready to run the Allagash River again!

David Leith

Wonderfully descriptive—a boy's outdoor adventure that leads to mature insights—a heartwarming ending.

Rosemary Ellis

Caught up in the story. You know your subject so well. It really involves the reader. I found your book very interesting and learned something from it.

George Robinette

ACKNOWLEDGMENTS

Heartfelt thanks to my mother and father for enabling me to experience nature.

Much appreciation to Carol Robinette, Caroline Meline, Andrea Tate, Moira Dean, David O'Brien, and Michael Leonard for their time and helpful editing suggestions.

DEDICATION

To all who seek to enjoy and preserve Earth's miraculous beauty.

TABLE OF CONTENTS

FOREWORD

The *Monarch of Tall Pines Pool* is an exciting adventure centered around a boy's and grandfather's quest for a trophy brook trout. When not pursuing their elusive quarry, Jeff and Gramps meet loon, osprey, beaver, bear, and other interesting animals. Fun-filled diversions include camping, canoeing, and climbing in the Adirondack Mountains.

Providing a vicarious getaway for the nature lover in us all, *The Monarch of Tall Pines Pool* will hopefully inspire readers to seek their own real-life adventures.

This book can be considered "Fact-Fiction": fact in that all events have been experienced by the author, fiction in that these experiences have been consolidated within a boy's week-long spring vacation. Furthermore, the fabled bear "Two Toes" is an enlarged representative of bears the author has seen in the wild.

Lastly, the story's protagonist—a trophy brook trout—replaces a huge carp that resided in a neighborhood pond.*

---

*For years, I enjoyed watching its glistening back plying the tranquil surface. Just once I fooled that monster; after a thrilling ten seconds, line and fish parted.

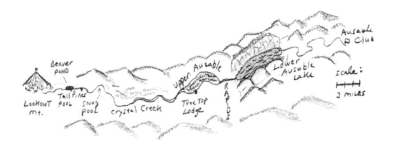

CHAPTER 1

DAY ONE:

THE TRIP BEGINS AT THE AUSABLE CLUB HOTEL

The boy woke early. Peering from a hotel window, sleepy eyes beheld a moonlit lake glimmering beneath forested mountains. Jeff was excited. He was in New York's Adirondack Mountains, about to enjoy spring vacation fishing, camping, and hiking with his grandfather. Their annual destination: the Ausable Wilderness Preserve—forty-thousand acres of lakes and forests abounding with beaver, bear, loon, and osprey.

Seeing these creatures in zoos was enjoyable, but observing them in the wild was a thrill.

Jeff's thoughts turned to fishing. He envisioned clear streams, rocky ravines, and mountain lakes. Nestled like jewels in a crown, their emerald depths promised to yield different treasure—*Brook trout.*

Jeff was eager to begin the adventure. *This trip had seemed forever in coming, but today had finally arrived!* Savoring the cool mountain air and contrasting warmth beneath the blankets, he stretched, rolled over, and glanced at the clock. Six a.m.—It was time to get up.

Jeff sprang out of bed, climbed into his dungarees, and put on a favorite flannel shirt. He then laced up his hiking boots, recently oiled and resoled for this occasion. Their soft, supportive leather felt good as he followed the grand sweep of the stairway down to the main hotel lobby.

The spacious room had tall bay windows bordered by tapestries and hardwood paneling. Old-time craftsmen had taken obvious pride in their workmanship. Though the historic hotel was also renowned for its professional staff and gourmet fare, Jeff was eager to leave catered civilization to enter a world where human conversation would be replaced by the call of the loon.

A vehicle arrived and Jeff sighted the familiar, smiling face of Jud Forster, his grandfather. The tall, lean man strode catlike across the lobby and lifted Jeff into the air amid happy hellos. After hugs and inquiries about family, Gramps got right down to business.

"Gear ready, lad?"

"Yes, Sir!"

"Well, Jeffrey, make yourself at home while I order our box lunches; I'll see you in the dining room shortly."

A large painting caught the boy's attention. A Winslow Homer watercolor, it depicted a fly fisherman casting over a mist-shrouded lake, backed by fall foliage. After admiring the impressive work, Jeff moved on.

He halted beneath a sizeable fish mounted over the dining room entranceway. Though nowhere near the bulk of deep-water monsters he'd seen in sporting magazines (forty-pound lake trout with spiked jaws and distended bellies), this smaller fish had a greater impact on him. Never had he seen a trout so large except at a fish hatchery where he had come upon an ancient hook-jawed brown trout residing in a breeder pen. What made the mounted fish so remarkable was that it was neither a brown nor a rainbow trout, both known to attain substantial size. According to the brass inscription, this was a *five-pound* brook trout.

Jeff studied its vermiculated back and shining body speckled crimson, yellow, and blue. *No wonder many considered this the peacock of freshwater fish!* He noted the triangular tail and orange pectoral and other fins shaped and positioned for maximum stability and propulsion. For several minutes, Jeff envisioned himself landing this prize. Then, with a sigh, he lowered his gaze and entered the dining room.

Jeff found his grandfather conversing at table-side with a friend, Mrs. Wilson. After greetings and introductions, the elders renewed their discussion.

The boy's thoughts continued with fishing. Periodic hometown outings for bluegills had been supplemented by a voracious love of outdoor journals. From these, one thing impressed him early on: "luck" came most to those best prepared; to hook and land fish regularly required skill. *What a reward a stringer of eight-inch trout would be, or a two-pounder, hefted before firelight and admiring friends!*

Jeff recalled the trout hatchery where ponds boiled with feeding fish. Wilderness trout had evolved a different look and temperament. Generations of selective breeding in the cold, clear streams had made wild fish as wary as they were beautiful.

Breakfast over, there was a shuffling of chairs as Gramps rose and gave his companion a farewell handshake. He then turned and smiled at Jeff.

"You wouldn't be wanting to leave soon now, would you, Jeffey-boy?"

His grandson grinned, nodded, and saluted.

"Aye, aye, Captain. Ready when you are!"

"Well, let's get on with it!" With arm across shoulder, Gramps escorted his grandson toward the lobby.

"How long does it take to get to your cabin?"

"About four hours, if the lakes aren't too rough."

The trip would be rigorous, regardless of the weather. A bumpy ten-mile drive preceded a four-mile paddle to the end of Lower Ausable Lake. Supplies would be portaged two miles to the Upper Lake and reloaded into a second canoe; a final three-mile paddle would bring them to his grandfather's rustic mountain camp overlooking the Upper Lake.

Jeff lingered beneath the archway for a final gaze at the big brook trout. He then stepped outside onto the sun-splashed veranda. Savoring a balsam-scented breeze, he scanned his surroundings. Majestic mountains rimmed the hotel grounds, creating a natural amphitheater.

A barn swallow flashed by. Adjusting its wings and tail, it veered in hot pursuit of a flying insect. Soon, it and other swallows were freewheeling through the sky like tiny jet fighters. Jeff admired the pretty, streamlined birds. Picking up his bags and fishing rod, he then headed toward the jeep.

"Son, give me a hand, will you please?" Gramps beckoned Jeff to the nearby boathouse. Among colorful rows of overturned canoes, Gramps pointed to his prized seventeen-footer. Lifting it from its storage bay, they walked it to the Jeep, and with synchronized grunts, placed it atop the vehicle's roof.

The canoe had been a gift from a grateful fishing client who, on his first outing with Gramps, had caught a trophy brook trout. Jeff's grandfather had politely declined the surprising offer, but when the canoe appeared on his front lawn the next morning, he decided to accept it in the spirit in which it was given. Slim, light, and durable, it suited Gramps's needs perfectly. Although not as strong as aluminum, its laminated wooden frame could yield enough to slide off most obstructions. Aluminum absorbed less shock and had a greater tendency to "stick" on rocks.

While Jeff held one end of the canoe, he watched his grandfather deftly tie the assorted knots needed to secure it.

With seventy-three years behind him, Gramps was still trim and athletic looking. Beneath a full mane of silver hair was a chiseled, well-tanned face, vigorous and sun-creased from exposure to the elements. Even now, his blue eyes seemed calm and deep like a mountain lake; his strong, even teeth shone white whenever he flashed his hearty smile. In short, he was an excellent example of a "sound mind, sound body." Gramps was a man who laughed easily and won the respect of all those fortunate to know him. There wasn't a person living in the Keene Valley who didn't respond positively when Jud Forster was mentioned.

"It's a long, bumpy ride in, Jeff, so make sure your side is secure."

To play it safe, Gramps came around and double-checked. It was this attention to detail that helped establish his enviable reputation of rarely repeating the same mistake.

One of Gramps's favorite expressions was "Attitude is everything." Indeed, his positive attitude was a prime factor in his remaining so vital and energetic.

"Let's go!" Gramps put the Jeep in gear, and with sprays of gravel, the two adventurers pulled onto the dirt road.

CHAPTER 2

GRAMPS DISCLOSES
AN EXCITING DISCOVERY

Soon, Jeff and his grandfather entered the Adirondack woods, still and silent. The emerald landscape was reminiscent of a lush rainforest; intermittent sunlight streaming through the high, swaying canopy illuminated mossy boulders, tree trunks, and dew-laden ferns.

Gramps downshifted the Jeep into creeper gear to climb a steep, rutted path snaking up the mountainside. Ten minutes later, they leveled off and rounded narrow hairpin turns bordering a precipitous ravine. Jeff heard running water. Peering over the brink, he spied a brook coursing the bottom of the chasm; the absence of guardrails made the view unsettling.

Hoping to distract his grandson, Gramps questioned how many million years it had taken water-propelled gravel to erode so deeply into such hard bedrock. The strategy worked; after learning some interesting geology, Jeff refocused on the swirling stream below. Where interrupted by boulders and jammed timbers, foamy pools had formed. In these, he hoped to spy the mysterious, wavering shadows of feeding trout.

"Gramps, how's the fishing been at camp?"

His grandfather's grin and gleaming eyes were answer enough.

"Gramps, you know that trout back at the hotel?"

"Biggest brookie ever taken from New York waters…caught by a client of mine back in '42. Some fish, eh?"

"You bet!…Gramps?"

"Yes, lad?"

"Do you think there are other fish that size around?"

Of all the inhabitants living in the valley, his grandfather was best qualified to answer. There were few fishermen more accomplished and respected than Gramps. His acute "fish sense," gained from forty years of guiding experience, had made him the man to see regarding local fishing matters. So when Jeff's question was met by silence, the boy was puzzled. He waited expectantly as Gramps narrowed his gaze and, surprisingly, halted the Jeep. Drawing in a deep breath and exhaling in a long, low whistle, he turned to Jeff.

"I was thinking you'd ask that question after seeing the hotel trout. I wanted to keep what I'm about to say a secret until later, but since you've brought up the subject..." Gramps paused, staring harder.

"Upstream from my cabin, I have come upon a brook trout so big... the hotel trout looks like its *baby* brother!"

Jeff was incredulous.

"You mean...?!"

Gramps nodded solemnly, his eyes showing fierce excitement.

Somewhere up Crystal Creek finned a monstrous brook trout—seldom seen, perhaps never hooked...WAITING TO BE CAUGHT!

It was hard to believe, but Gramps's reputation had not been gained by fabricating fish stories. *Somehow, what he was saying must be true.*

Still, Jeff challenged, "I've never heard of fish that size around here. How do you know?"

Before speaking, Gramps paused to compose himself for what he knew would sound like a very tall tale. Had it been anyone but his grandson, he would have kept silent.

CHAPTER 3

JEFF LEARNS ABOUT "KING"— THE MONARCH OF TALL PINES POOL

Gramps started by saying, "The locals will tell you this fish doesn't exist. Yet two years ago, I was casting at a special place where the creek spills ten feet into a deep, clear pool."

He produced a hand-drawn map from the glove compartment. Opening it, he pointed to a notated spot on Crystal Creek.

"Tall Pines Pool?"

"That's the place!" Gramps continued, "From a fisherman's standpoint, this was the most promising looking water I had ever encountered. In fact, this pool had always yielded a nice catch of eight to ten-inch fish, so imagine my puzzlement when a half-dozen casts aroused no action.

"It was late afternoon, and long shadows were beginning to fall. A setting sun was filtering through the trees, and I was about to pack up when I happened to look at the deep center pool. What I saw still gives me the shakes…

"A shadowy form began rising like a submarine through the depths. It was so large, I figured it had to be a piece of driftwood. But when it neared the surface—*THIS was no driftwood!* Above the water wavered a three-inch fin; below, spots glowed like jewels; at the broad, tapered end, I saw an eye!

"I wondered if the long hours and afternoon sun were playing tricks on me. But there it was, resting on the surface…it was a trout all right, but WHAT a trout! It was a giant brook trout, and here I was frozen like a hunter with 'buck fever,' too fascinated to do anything but stand and admire my extraordinary discovery."

Jeff stared at his grandfather, wide-eyed and open-mouthed.

Gramps went on: "I watched the fish's immense gills working. White and scarlet flashed as it opened and shut its spiked mouth. For several minutes, it lingered with pectorals flared, trailing a V-shaped riffle. Then the creature began to move, allowing the current to carry it on a slow, downstream drift.

"I stood immobilized as it approached. Now I had a clear view of its wolf-like head facing upstream, watching everything drifting before its cold-staring eyes. It reached the shallows, fanning its tail just enough to stabilize its ponderous weight. A few seconds more and I could've touched the trout's broad mossy back. Incredibly, its leathery tail flicked my boot… an explosion of spray, a blurred streak…then, nothing…nothing but water gurgling past me.

"I don't know how long I stood in a trance; the raucous 'clack-clacking' of a kingfisher finally reminded me it was getting dark and time to head home."

Jeff's grandfather paused to enjoy his grandson's anticipated reaction.

Seeing the boy transfixed with mute anticipation, Gramps was quick to oblige.

"Needless to say, my discovery left me ecstatic. When I reached home, your Grandmom noticed something unusual. But I wanted to keep my discovery a secret until the time I might lay this monster on our table and enjoy the look on her face!"

Jeff's mind reeled with questions: *Where had the trout come from? Why had it acted the way it did?*

Gramps continued.

"Here was the chance to fulfill my lifelong goal of landing a truly extraordinary trout. One thing was sure: The fish I had come upon could well be the biggest brook trout ever to reside in New York waters.

"Now that 'my' fish had been found, there remained the challenge of capturing it. I began plotting my strategy.

"First, I chose and inspected my tackle. I oiled my fly reel and refilled it with premium sinking line. Now an important consideration: Should I tie on a four- pound test leader and risk it being seen, or should I stay with my usual two-pound test monofilament, which promised more strikes but had obvious disadvantages against heavy fish in rock-filled shallows? I chose the stronger line, then selected a half-dozen hand-tied flies.

"Now for the proper rod. I immediately reached for my old favorite—a seven-foot 'Orvis,' custom made of bamboo. It was perfectly balanced, sensitive throughout the tip, and its laminated construction gave it enough backbone to tire fish of some size and power. But would it be enough to handle THIS fish?"

Gramps rested his voice while memories stirred his features.

"The next morning, I was up before dawn. I dressed and quietly crept out the door. When I arrived at Tall Pines Pool, sunlight streamed through the trees, illuminating rocks and water. The pool was so clear, only a crouch and slow cast might have prevented the fish from spooking.

"I cast out to the main current. As my fly floated downstream, I waited nervously…nothing happened.

"Why didn't the trout strike? How could it have allowed my choice morsel to drift by?

"I aimed my second cast slightly to the right. When the current carried the nymph into slack water near the pool's end, I again retrieved it. Growing uneasy, I cast once more. Then again and again, and still again. Fifteen minutes later, I sat upon a stream-side boulder to ponder my next move.

"Jeff, I began to question whether this fish really existed. My mind told me 'yes'... *yesterday, I had seen a monster trout in this very pool.* Yet, today!

"Might he have moved downstream? The falls were a formidable barrier. Though Tall Pines Pool was an ideal haunt, the brookie's appetite probably required it to swim downstream in search of minnows, crayfish, and nymphs."

Unable to contain himself, Jeff broke in, "Where is the trout now? Is it still alive?"

"It's hard to say." Gramps's voice seemed tinged with sadness, and his face showed a distant look of dreams unfulfilled. Then he brightened again.

"We'll check a couple of prime spots and see if the ol' boy's hanging out. One thing's certain: he was there last year, so I'll wager he's still upstream…" Gramps's voice lowered, "with my fly still stuck in his jaw."

"You mean…you *hooked* him?"

His grandfather nodded, eyes narrowed and intent.

Jeff's eyes were saucers. *To have battled this huge brook trout!* What had started as a routine fishing trip had escalated into a bigger quest.

CHAPTER 4

THE PADDLE; LOON CHASE

The jeep now traveled up a pronounced incline. Rounding numerous turns, they climbed toward the mountain's lofty summit.

"Wait'll you see the view!"

When they reached the mountaintop, Gramps parked the Jeep. Jeff jumped out and strode to a scenic outlook. Sweeping his gaze, he took in the panorama of wilderness.

Far below lay the quicksilver waters of a mountain lake, flanked by towering walls of granite. A lone hawk soared the heights. Barely discernable as it patrolled in relaxed loops, its outstretched wings caught the thermals rising from sun-warmed rocks below.

It was a gusty day. The lake surface was whitened by wind blowing in their direction; Gramps's resigned expression forewarned the difficulty of the upcoming paddle.

Descending the steep, rutted road, Jeff was forced to cling to the lurching vehicle. A final jolting turn brought them to lake's edge. Gramps parked the Jeep, shut off the motor, and Jeff exited.

Ahhhh! What relief to stretch his legs! After exploring his surroundings, he donned his life-jacket and helped transport Gramps's canoe to the dock. As they were sliding the unstable craft into the lake, a barrage of unruly waves began smacking it.

Supplies were quickly but carefully loaded. Gramps then maneuvered the bow into the wind and held the dock rope while his companion climbed in and took position in the bow.

As Gramps pushed off, he was knocked off balance by a surging broadside wave; by the time he recovered, the drifting boat was approaching menacing rocks and timbers littering the shoreline.

"Ready?"

Jeff barely heard his grandfather above the wind. Instinctively, he leaned over the gunwale and plunged his paddle into the lake. As he powered through strokes, he enjoyed conquering the resisting water. This pleasure soon faded as the low-riding craft was continuously pounded by heavy waves.

Gramps shouted for his bowman to kneel.

"Gives you best leverage for paddling and lessens wind resistance." He added, "You can also reduce wind drag by flattening your paddle on the upswing of each stroke."

They leaned forward in their seats. "Str-o-o-o-ke…str-o-o-o-ke…str-o-o-o-ke!" Both labored in synchronized movements to make headway in the driving wind. Their strained efforts generated slow but gradual momentum; still, Jeff was disheartened observing the almost stationary shoreline.

Onward they struggled. Random waves peaked and poured overboard until four inches of water sloshed about the canoe bottom. Taking time for bailing would forfeit hard-fought ground, but there was no alternative. Jeff asked why they had set out under such adverse conditions.

Gramps pointed to an expanded line of clear sky promising better conditions; in the meantime, he felt his grandson might benefit from being exposed to a challenging "bit of weather."

To maintain a direct route, they set their bearings on a distant peninsula. While this strategy helped, twenty minutes of hard paddling still found them frustratingly far from their target. Yet, their landmark grew imperceptibly; at long last, they wearily drew alongside its offshore boulders.

"Break time!"

With Gramps's welcome words, the two slumped over their paddles. The point's leeward side offered some protection from the buffeting wind; here the voyagers caught their breath and shared a candy bar. Such luxuries were short-lived, however, for soon they were squinting and paddling in search of a new landmark.

Feelings of accomplishment were quickly over-ridden by feelings of fatigue; Jeff's only respite came in the brief moments between strokes.

"Whew!" He recalled a favorite saying of his wrestling coach: "When the going gets tough, the tough get going." Just when he could labor no more, Jeff reached a curious state of "second-wind" when his muscles felt somewhat recovered. He welcomed this period of relative relief. *But for how long?*

Jeff was cold, his bones ached, his teeth chattered and his knuckles were raw and scraped, but purposefully, almost mechanically, he struggled onward. There was no use sulking or complaining. His father had encouraged making the most of every situation.

With renewed determination, Jeff clamped down on his paddle and drove it back into the windswept chop. Str-o-o-o-ke...str-o-o-o-ke. It helped knowing that each burning sensation brought him closer to his destination. Silently they pushed past the halfway point. Jeff hoped the final leg would be easier. Even while thinking this, he felt a perceptible change in the wind. Whereas it had been whipping across in a nonstop blow, it was now moving in reduced, sporadic gusts. Looking to the horizon, their weary eyes welcomed an enlarged patch of blue sky. The improved weather gave cause for celebration.

Break time!

Jeff had been working so hard he hadn't noticed his enormous thirst. Reaching for his canteen, he heard Gramps chuckle.

"Try the lake, son. You won't taste any better."

"You mean all this water is safe to drink?"

His grandfather gave Jeff a smiling go-ahead. While Gramps balanced the craft, his grandson leaned over the side and cautiously took a sip.

This mountain water was as fine tasting as any known drink, totally unlike the chemically treated stuff running from the tap back home!

As he took long, refreshing gulps, Jeff felt grateful for this lake's millions of gallons of clear, cold, drinkable water. Finally, he sat up, wiped his chin, and viewed the isolated grandeur of his surroundings.

What a primitive-looking place! The nearby shoreline was littered with huge chunks of weathered granite dislodged over eons from the cliffs above. Repeated freezing and thawing had created cracks in the stone; in winter, water in these cracks froze and expanded, exerting enough pressure to enlarge the cracks. Over time, chunks would break free and crash down, thunderously sweeping everything in their path.

Jeff squinted upward and viewed a line of stunted trees silhouetted atop the thousand-foot summit. He wondered how they could exist in such inhospitable barrens. Anchored by clutching roots, many pines angled off the cliff walls.

The paddlers continued down the lake. After rounding a bend, Gramps called out, "Look at that loon and her baby!"

Jeff sighted along his pointed finger, only to gaze at open water. "Where?"

"They're gone. Loons dive whenever they sense danger."

The birds popped to the surface moments later.

Gramps said, "If the mother were alone, you still wouldn't see her. I've seen adults travel a couple hundred yards before resurfacing."

Jeff had learned these large birds were fish-eaters adept at overtaking their fast-swimming quarry. Evolution had progressively moved their webbed feet back to afford maximum propulsion. Loons had become so adapted to water that they rarely ventured onto land, except when nesting.

18

By now, the mother and baby were hastily paddling off to a safer distance.

Gramps preferred not disturbing wild creatures, but offered an exception for educational purposes.

"Want to catch the baby?"

Jeff nodded eagerly and a short chase ensued. The frantic mother tried diverting the pursuer's attention by feigning disablement—a sometimes effective trick practiced by certain species. As she thrashed off in an opposite direction, hoping to lure the "danger" toward herself, the youngster was quickly scooped into the canoe. Jeff fondled the peeping baby a minute or two, enjoying the experience. He then leaned over and allowed it to reunite with its anxiously patrolling mother.

The wind had died and the sun grew warmer. Suddenly, the morning quiet was broken by a loud shout and its echo.

In a split second, Gramps's voice had sped to and from the far cliffs. Jeff yelled several times, delighting in the clarity of his own echoes.

CHAPTER 5

END OF THE FIRST PADDLE; FROGS, TURTLES AND DRAGONFLIES

A quarter mile up the lake was Ice Cave, a favorite landmark. Just offshore, a house-sized boulder loomed above drifting mist. Beneath its cave-like base, the lake bed plunged eighty feet; the deeper water here maintained a temperature around fifty degrees. In winter, many fish congregated in its relative warmth; conversely, in summer, they sought the higher oxygen levels found in its then cooler depths.

Dissolved minerals from underwater springs encouraged the growth of microorganisms constituting the first essential link in the lake's food chain. Because each level of life benefitted from increased populations preceding it, the fishing at Ice Cave was usually outstanding.

Even now, a small boat was drifting about the area. It belonged to the McDonnells, on their way home from their Upper Lake camp. Gramps's voice broke the silence.

"Any luck?"

Jack McDonnell grinned as he held up a good-sized fish. It was a brook trout, resplendent in its native colors.

"Nice going, Mac!"

Jeff loved eating these fish pan-fried, with crisp skin and tender pink flesh.

After the McDonnells left the area, the newcomers tried deep trolling with colorful streamers, but with no success. Further action at Ice Cave would have to wait.

Following a short paddle, Jeff and his grandfather entered a narrow inlet bordered by dense alder thickets. Gramps stood to better navigate the rock-filled shallows; occasionally, the laden canoe scraped bottom. When grounded, its occupants leaned hard against their paddles and rocked the boat free.

Rounding the final bend, they glided over a sandbar into the sanctuary of a small cove dotted with lily pads. On the far shore stood the boathouse, marking the lake's end and the termination of their first and hardest paddle.

The cove brimmed with life. The unexpected arrival of human beings touched off a chorus of croaks as numerous frogs dove for the safety of the mud bottom.

Three painted turtles, stacked like pancakes, toppled off their favorite sunning log. Comic confusion had erupted when the uppermost turtles, lacking footholds, futilely clawed air until undermined by their diving brethren.

After the turtles slipped from view, the frogs became bolder. One by one they resurfaced, until a dozen bulbous eyes protruded above the waterline in watchful vigilance.

Beneath the tranquil surface, a leopard frog rhythmically kicked its muscular legs, propelling itself in smooth, lengthy glides.

Gramps and Jeff disembarked at the boathouse dock. Unloading the canoe, they carried it into the shed and lifted it onto a storage rack. They then sat down and enjoyed a breather and a sandwich.

Dragonflies were darting about the cove. Two small species were admired—one with iridescent blue wings, the other a vibrant green.

Seemingly inspecting the strangers was a larger variety with spotted wings. Harmless to humans, it was a voracious hunter capable of consuming hundreds of mosquitoes daily. Now the dragonfly hovered like a helicopter, its blurred wings fanning a hundred beats per second, its large multi-lensed eyes enabling it to see simultaneously in all directions. Watching the large insect rattle off, the boy was thankful this ubiquitous "bomber" of the lowlands no longer possessed the two and a half foot wing span of its prehistoric predecessors.

Jeff was helped into his back pack. With fifty pounds pulling against his shoulders, some adjustment was needed before beginning the two-mile portage to the Upper Lake.

"No use carrying these longer than we have to—let's march!" announced Gramps.

CHAPTER 6

THE CARRY AND INLAND JOURNEY TO TREE TOP LODGE; "TWO TOES"

Gramps led the way onto a narrow trail entering the woods. Both hikers concentrated on the uneven stony path, latticed with roots. In time, Jeff stopped to readjust his pack digging into paddle-sore shoulders. He thought about the area's early settlers: *though small in stature, French Canadians supposedly jogged much of their lengthy portages bearing up to 180 pounds of gear!*

Entering an old stand of white pines, they enjoyed walking upon its spongy carpet of fallen needles. The grove's towering canopy and dimly lit column-like trunks inspired feelings of being in a huge, quiet cathedral.

Beyond the pines, the trail opened to a sunlit meadow alive with buzzing insects and chirping birds. Here was a world profuse with wildflowers, ferns, and white birch. Jeff traversed a square-hewn tree trunk spanning a sparkling brook. Midway across, he paused to follow the distinctive flight of a flicker. Soon, the woods resonated with its "tat-a-tat-tat-tat" as the woodpecker hopped about the vertical remains of a beech tree. Hammering in evenly spaced rows, it used its barbed tongue to spear beetles and grubs hiding beneath the bark.

Now the flicker's host became the subject of the boy's inexhaustible curiosity. Most beech trees have smooth, silver-gray trunks supporting full-foliaged crowns, but this particular specimen had lost its top. Since there were no vertical scars on the trunk indicating damage from lightning, Jeff surmised this tree had been besieged by carpenter ants. His theory was borne out by the fallen section, whose base was riddled with a labyrinth of ant borings. In a strong wind, the tree had snapped at its weakest point. The gaping, uppermost cavity was now surrounded by new growth.

Jeff circled the tree and spoke excitedly, "Gramps! What're these?"

A series of one- to three-inch scars spiraled up the trunk. Gramps confirmed Jeff's guess.

"Bear claw marks…neat! More'n likely a black bear was looking for honey in that hollow."

Jeff, now on the far side of the beech tree, excitedly beckoned to his grandfather.

"Gramps, look at THESE!"

The boy stood rigid, pointing to an unusual set of claw marks. The deeply indented, oversized scars were identified as having been made by the legendary "Two Toes." Exceeding 600 pounds, it was the largest black bear known to have roamed these parts.

"Gosh!" Jeff looked around uneasily, but relaxed when his grandfather assured him the great bear no longer lived.

"Even if he did, you'd stand little chance of being endangered. As a rule, wild animals are more interested in avoiding you than you are in avoiding them. Usually, a bear's acute senses of hearing and smell enable him to detect your presence and leave the area long before you ever see him."

"Tell me more about Two Toes."

"OK lad, but we'll start with a question: Do you know why it's usually not good to feed wild animals?"

"Because they can get lazy?"

"Right you are, Jeffrey! Then what happens?"

"They get spoiled, so that when winter comes and humans aren't around, the animals not used to getting their own food have a hard time surviving."

"Right again. Very good!" Gramps continued, "Now, Two Toes became a victim of just such circumstances. For years, he had roamed the

Adirondack countryside, foraging for berries and turning over logs and stones for tasty ants, grubs, and field mice. He would eat all he could, so that by fall he would have built up a thick layer of fat. This would keep him warm and supply his body with stored-up energy during the winter months when he was hibernating."

Gramps explained that, while in deep sleep, the bear's metabolic rate would slow to where its body could subsist on its fat alone. In springtime, the hungry bear would emerge from his den to again become Lord of the Woodlands.

According to Gramps, careless campers had left garbage strewn about camp. Old Two Toes had caught its scent and quickly became spoiled by the easier life it afforded. It was only a matter of time before he fell into the unsociable habit of digging up garbage dumps and smashing food storage shelters to keep up with his newly advanced standard of living. Plans were made to capture the bear and transport him elsewhere, but bounty hunters illegally set a trap into which the unfortunate bruin stepped. In a desperate act of self-preservation, he must have struggled mightily to free himself, but in so doing, he left three toes behind.

"Now you know how he got his name," said Gramps. "For two more seasons, the bear remained at large. Finally, the next spring, when he emerged groggy from his winter lair, he lumbered into the camouflaged cage we had constructed. After the great bear was sedated with a dart, he was airlifted by helicopter 150 miles to a sparsely populated relocation site and released."

"What happened then?" Jeff leaned forward in anticipation.

"All was peaceful the next three weeks," Gramps continued. "Then one day I was amazed to come across fresh spoor bearing the unmistakable trademark of the animal I had come to know so well. Soon after, an incoming party's food cache was ransacked. Old Two Toes was back!

"How he had found his way across all those miles of unfamiliar terrain, I'll never know. It was as mysterious and fascinating to me as how birds migrate thousands of miles or how oceanic salmon unfailingly find the exact fresh water stream in which they were born four years before.

"Something had to be done. I suggested another entrapment, but the first had proved unsuccessful and the townspeople were becoming increasingly alarmed. Unhappily, I was overruled. Yet, how could I destroy a creature whom I had grown to respect and who had as much right to remain in this back country as I did?"

Jeff's brow wrinkled as he awaited the outcome of the story.

"It was a sad day when I was given official orders to do away with Two Toes," sighed Gramps. "I almost refused, but one day I had no choice, as I came upon the great beast badly wounded by a poacher's gun. Half-blind and confused, he must have thought I was the source of his suffering. As I prepared to put him out of his misery, he charged, snorting and snarling. I managed to fire one hasty shot, praying the single bullet would be enough to stop this fur-covered locomotive before he raked me over. His momentum carried him within yards of my feet, and there he collapsed like a huge sleeping dog."

Gramps concluded by expressing his sorrow in having lost so grand a creature, then noted, "His pelt now hangs above my hearth in fond remembrance."

Jeff looked at his grandfather intently. "And all that started because someone carelessly left food out?"

"That's right, Jeff. I hope you've learned a lesson."

———————— · ————————

When Jeff and Gramps approached the next bend, the musical tinkling of the stream became more audible. Downstream, its sound intensified to a reverberating roar. Jeff looked in awe at the torrent rushing over boulders.

"Where does all this water come from?"

"It's the runoff from the Upper Ausable Lake…some flow, eh?"

"Boy, how about canoeing THOSE rapids!"

"You'll get your chance later," Gramps assured. "I've run this stretch when the water was even higher; believe me, you can't underestimate the current's power!"

They traveled past the wildest section until the roar subsided. Beyond lay shimmering open water; they were approaching the Upper Ausable Lake.

Now, a pleasant choice: *should they follow a side path to picnic at Shanty Brook or continue on to base camp?* Gramps considered the time and the lake's increased choppiness.

"We'd better keep going, but first let's take a breather."

Jeff whistled a relieved *"Whew!"* as he let the heavy pack slide off his aching shoulders. After resting atop the boathouse dock, he arose and made a few casts.

"Jud Forster, good afternoon!" It was Mr. McCabe, forest ranger and Gramps's longtime friend. "Guess you and I are the only ones up here right now," he said jovially.

"Just the way we like it! How's the fishing?" asked Gramps.

"Been pretty good, Jud." Mr. McCabe turned to Jeff. "Keep it up, son. You never know when you might latch on to a good one."

He pointed to where Jeff was standing. "Last week a three-pound brookie was caught right here. Might've lived under the dock and no one knew it."

Jeff hastily cast. After a half-dozen retrieves, he asked about their chances of seeing a bear.

"There's a healthy population up here. One's been sighted around the dump, so you'll want to be extra careful burying your garbage."

Before departing, Mr. McCabe offered, "I'm heading to the old Anderson camp…like a tow?"

Grins creased tired faces; a tow was a rare luxury, for the ranger's motorboat was the only one allowed on the lake.

They slid the canoe into the water and Mr. McCabe fastened his tow rope to its bow. Starting his motor, he increased the throttle and the canoe began slicing through the windy chop.

"Boy, this is living!" Jeff chuckled appreciatively. He imagined he was on a nineteenth-century Nantucket "Sleigh Ride," enjoying an exhilarating speed tow behind a rampaging, harpooned whale.

Above the narrow shoreline, thick forests extended up steep mountainsides. In the distance, a waterfall cascaded five hundred feet down a cliff. Sunlight passing through its veil of spray created a beautiful spectral arc—*the most magnificent rainbow Jeff had ever seen!* They drifted through its invigorating mist.

Finally, they rounded the third point.

"There's the camp dock!" Jeff shouted.

High up the mountainside, Gramps's rustic Tree Top Lodge was all but hidden by evergreens; tendrils of wafting smoke revealed its location.

When the voyagers arrived at dockside, Jeff tossed the towline to Mr. McCabe. After securing the canoe, they thanked the ranger, shook hands, and bid farewell.

"See you gents later...have fun!" With that, Mr. McCabe motored off, growing smaller before vanishing around the point.

CHAPTER 7

ARRIVAL AT TREE TOP LODGE

"Look who's here to greet us!"

The box turtle Gramps found had a shell patterned with bright yellow and brown hexagons. When picked up, the creature hissed and withdrew its head and legs into its armored home.

Jeff knew its hinged under-shell could shut so tightly that a predator swatting it around would often become frustrated and move on. The turtle was presently adopting this strategy; after a minute of quiet, it slowly extended its head with red eyes peering.

When re-handled, it withdrew its appendages with another dull *snap*. The turtle repeated this behavior until acclimated enough to try "swimming" out of Jeff's hands.

These reptiles were the longest lived of all animals. This particular specimen might live one hundred years, while its slow-moving 500-pound cousin, the Galapagos tortoise, could survive an additional fifty.

The record holders in nature's longevity contest were certain trees. The big Adirondack pines had been growing some 250 years, but these were mere youngsters compared to a 4,600-year-old bristlecone pine inhabiting the windswept barrens of California's Sierra Nevada Mountains. In National Geographic, Jeff had seen pictures of these goblin-like trees, with twisted trunks like sand-polished driftwood. Serpentine strips of living bark, ascending to bleached branches, nurtured random tufts of green needles.

The region's extreme aridity contributed to the bristlecone's longevity; with little ground cover, damaging brush fires were almost nonexistent. Borings of growth rings examined under a microscope had shown bristlecone trunks growing as little as one inch in two hundred years!

Jeff refocused on the rustic dwelling situated one hundred feet up the steep mountainside. Wearily trudging up the zigzagging path, he and his grandfather climbed the wooden steps leading to a spacious, covered porch. There to greet them was Jeff's grandmother.

"Welcome to Tree Top Lodge!"

After she hugged and conversed with her grandson, Ma Forster, as she was known, asked Jeff to make himself at home before excusing herself. "Have to quick-check the oven."

"Can I help you with anything?" Jeff asked.

Jeff's grandmother smiled. "You and Jud can help yourselves to dinner in just a while. Thanks for offering!"

Jeff walked over to a high wicker chair and gratefully sat. Gazing over acres of evergreens to the lake below, he felt he was in a giant tree fort. *Tree Top Lodge—what an appropriate name!*

Feeling drowsy, he made his way to the guide's quarters adjoining the kitchen. There, he found a cot and soon dozed off.

———————— · ————————

Jeff awoke to the setting sun casting a golden glow over the lake and mountains beyond. He thought about his great-grandfather who had settled in this area a century ago. On this mountainside, the man had cleared land and hewn the long, straight timbers with which he built this impressive structure. It had remained his beloved home—the place where he had raised Jeff's grandfather and taught him the ways of the woods. Here, Gramps had learned to respect all living things and to keep the area as unspoiled as when he had first come upon it.

Jeff spied a plump spider descending from a gossamer thread attached to an upper porch eave. As Jeff watched, this artful engineer spun a web that, for beauty and function, was one of nature's finest forms.

The spider began the web by climbing upwind and spinning out a continuous stream of silk. This was carried by air currents until it reached and stuck to a distant support. The spider crawled along this "tightrope" while spinning a second anchor line for added reinforcement. Next, a parallel thread was spun a couple of feet below. The outside border was completed by two vertical connecting threads.

Now, without pause or distraction, the spider climbed halfway along the upper strand and dropped down onto the lower parallel. Then pulling itself back up, it stopped midway and began playing out a new strand kept parallel by means of an outstretched leg. After many repetitions, the web took on the appearance of a spoked wheel. Up until now, the threads were non-sticky ones, permitting easy mobility. From here on, the spider began to spin a sticky circular pattern, starting at the spoked center and gradually expanding outward. When the spider had finally completed its net, it climbed beneath the eave to await a victim.

Manual jiggling of the web would not fool the spider, for it could detect the difference between such counterfeit motion and vibrations made by a struggling insect.

If the web trapped a large wasp or other insect too big and strong for the spider's liking, the latter would fearlessly descend. Rather than tangle with the desperate adversary, the spider would neatly cut around its captive. Letting the insect fall free, the spider would move in to repair the damage.

Smaller insects would be bitten by the spider and, in seconds, the injected venom would paralyze the prey. In this state of suspended animation, the insect might be wrapped and stored for a fresh meal later on.

The dinner gong sounded. An old locomotive wheel, it clanged sonorously when struck by a sledgehammer. The sky was still ablaze as Jeff followed the breezeway back to the dining quarters.

He entered the dining room and hungrily surveyed the spread: roast wild goose with apricot-raisin sauce, potatoes, peas, homemade bread, and apple cider.

"Yummm!" Jeff rubbed his belly. "Smells as good as it looks!"

He sat with his grandparents and began savoring the first of several heaping portions, thinking this was *some* way to rough it! When done, he thanked and complimented his grandmother for the splendid feast.

"Can I help with the dishes?"

She happily accepted his offer, looking forward to the chance to further chat with her grandson.

Afterward, Jeff sought out a comfortable couch in the main living room. Coals from a fire still glowed in the walk-in fireplace. Its light and that from flickering wall candles softly illuminated the room. Amid the pulsating shadows, his gaze fell upon a huge and glossy bear pelt spanning a timber wall.

Two Toes! Jeff studied the bear's massive head—its yellow eyes reflecting a fiery glint, its jaws packed with a formidable set of ivory teeth. He felt its claws protruding like brandished daggers from out of heavy, powerful paws. Several toes were missing. Jeff would have loved seeing this magnificent creature alive, but touching it in this living room was thrill enough.

Although he had never known Charles Forster, his great-grandfather who had built and inhabited this magnificent lodge, there was much in the room's design and furnishings that gave Jeff insight into its original owner.

Despite its spacious size and lofty ceiling, the room was cozy. Like a museum, it held many artifacts and much evidence of the owner's love for the outdoors. Even the wood and leather furniture had been made by Jeff's great-grandfather. A library of books, including hand-inscribed volumes containing diverse wood-lore, filled the side wall.

Mounted behind glass was an impressive display of Iroquois arrowheads found by Gramps's father exploring the area's stream beds and ancient paths. Charlie Forster was a foremost authority on these former inhabitants of the Keene Valley. Jeff looked forward to learning more about these and other Indian tribes; his grandfather clearly held them in great respect. They had been a proud people holding trust and honor in highest regard who had lived in close harmony with their surroundings.

Aside from being a noted author, woodsman, woodworker, historian, and humanitarian, Charles Forster had been a taxidermist of considerable skill. Evidence of his work was displayed throughout the cabin. A handsome whitetail deer head was mounted on a plaque over the fireplace. The buck's broad rack had twelve tines—a splendid specimen.

A colorful wood duck, poised in flight, was affixed to the stand of a table lamp. Another of Jeff's favorite birds, a male ring-neck pheasant, was mounted to best display its varied patterns and iridescent colors. Over the master bedroom door hung a four-pound brook trout, caught years ago at Ice Cave. The sight of the full-bodied fish renewed Jeff's interest in Gramps's tale about his encounter with the trout at Tall Pines Pool.

Making his way outside, he followed a narrow footpath toward a glow visible through the trees. Soon he entered a small clearing where the darkened forms of his grandparents sat silhouetted before a roaring campfire. Gramps stirred the hot coals, sending a shower of sparks swirling up into the cool night air.

"Howdy, pardner! Just in time for a bedtime snack." Gramps's hearty laugh welcomed Jeff.

He handed the boy an opened bag of marshmallows. Jeff broke a branch from a nearby sapling and whittled a point with his pocket knife. Skewering four marshmallows, he rotated them over the coals. When their outside crusts turned crisp golden brown, they were ready to be popped in the mouth, yielding their sweet, melted core.

After enjoying his fill, Jeff sat and stared at the ever-changing flames. He listened to the hiss and crackle of gasses and moisture escaping from the wood. When he stirred the coals, ribbon-like trails of sparks surged into the sky, popping like fireworks. Along with friends, food, and shelter, a campfire was one of life's basic pleasures. Ahhhh…*It was good to be here!*

Ma Forster stood up, stretched, and bade her husband and grandson goodnight. She then turned to the path leading to the lodge and disappeared among the trees.

Gramps addressed Jeff: "We'll be heading out early, so we better get some shut-eye."

His grandson protested. "What about the trout? You promised to finish your story!"

Gramps chuckled slyly and winked.

"Didn't think you'd remember...Actually, I thought tomorrow might be a better time, because what you'll hear might make you restless all night."

In response to his grandson's pleading, Gramps finally succumbed.

"But don't say I didn't warn you. Now, where were we?"

"You said you hooked the brook trout!"

"Ah...yes..." Gramps's voice trailed away as if overtaken by a yearning memory.

CHAPTER 8

GRAMPS CONTINUES
HIS STORY ABOUT THE TROUT

"For weeks, I searched for the trout. One day, while walking the path above Snag Pool, I approached a favorite section where the stream widens and glides glass-smooth over sand and eelgrass. This stretch had always nurtured good hatches, and that day the surface was massed with struggling insects.

"Something seemed out of place, but I couldn't put my finger on it. Curious, I lingered until my peripheral vision sighted a movement in midstream. I squinted into the glare, but saw nothing. After more waiting, I was about to continue on when a glistening hump broke surface, then slipped from view.

"'What *WAS* that?'

"Soon it reappeared, but was gone again.

"On its third appearance, it remained—its extraordinary length cleaving a trailing riffle.

41

"I felt like cheering, but didn't dare. It was MY TROUT!

"With eyes riveted on midstream, I slowly dropped on all fours and crept up the weed-choked path. I had hoped to get a closer look, but was dismayed when the fish again sank from sight. Had my movements spooked it?

"Holding my breath, I shifted out of the glare and put on sunglasses. With the surface glare eliminated, I could see its great speckled form resting on the bottom. Then it began to rise. A new hatch had begun.

"From my vantage point, I studied the trout's feeding habits. As a struggling fly floated down, the fish's pectorals flared and fanned in increasing tempo. With a soundless sweep, it propelled itself upward, curling its tail as it moved to intercept its approaching quarry. When its broad snout came within inches of the fly, its gills distended, jaws opened, and the bug was inhaled in a gulp of water. Closing its mouth and expelling water through its gills, it sank to its former lie and resumed the slow fanning of its fins."

Gramps paused long enough to enjoy Jeff's excitement. Then, he continued.

"The trout rarely ventured sideways to intercept a passing insect. While larvae were hatching, it seemed interested only in those floaters drifting overhead. Moreover, the fish showed a preference for only one species of fly, disdaining two larger varieties that dimpled the surface by the hundreds. Often, it would allow several identical insects to pass before eagerly slurping up the next.

"The trout was becoming more playful. Thrashing from one feeding station to another, it plowed the water as it gorged on insects." Gramps paused to look at the campfire, clearly enjoying the memory of the feeding trout. Then he went on.

"I thought about my useless collection of wet flies. I was determined to try for him anyway and cast a counterfeit, but, predictably, the fish showed no interest. No longer able to stand the helplessness of the situation, I headed home. There, I selected a number of flies resembling the midges the trout had preferred. I hoped that by my return, he wouldn't have changed his menu. To ensure matching the hatch, I brought extra flies.

"As cooler evening approached, I headed my canoe back up Crystal Creek. My surroundings became orchestrated with conversing crickets and peeping tree frogs. A luna moth fluttered by, sporting velvet-green wings and fern-like antennae. Several bats swept the sky."

Jeff interrupted, wanting to know how these flying mammals could track and capture insects at night. Gramps explained that bats had evolved sensory systems similar to radar. In flight, they emit continuous high-pitched squeaks echoing back to their huge ears and convoluted noses.

How bats could process these echoes in time to chase and capture flying insects was incomprehensible.

Gramps noticed Jeff's face reflecting interest in resuming the tale. He continued:

"I paddled hurriedly to allow enough daylight for my mission. Hopefully, the hatch would still be on; I did not want to spend another month on this quest.

"Leaving the slow water of Snag Pool, I drifted around the bend and searched upstream. *Nothing.* I waited—then I saw the telltale ripple. *The trout was still there and feeding! But for how long?* I felt reassured, for during hatches, fish often continue eating after their gullets are overflowing.

"I nervously cast upstream. My fly settled above the waiting fish. *So far, so good!* As the drifting counterfeit approached the trout, my excitement grew. I saw the dorsal fin move forward. *The trout was interested!* When it's broad snout was only inches from the fly, the monster began drifting backward, eyeing it. During those long seconds, the suspense was unbearable. *Had the moment arrived?*

"Suddenly, the trout lost interest and sank from view.

"*Robbed!* I quickly reeled in. A tiny twig had caught the leader, dragging the fly enough to spook this wary fish. *Of all the luck!*

"Fearing I had blown my chances, I glanced up, relieved to find the trout not only still there, but back in business.

"I forced myself to wait him out one...two...three endless minutes. Finally, I *had* to cast.

"As my drifting fly approached the trout's predicted location, my body tensed and eyes strained. I saw the moonlit surface ripple as the fish sipped the fly, then pulled my rod down into an impossible arc.

"Line now tore from my reel as King torpedoed across the pool, plowing the surface to foam. Rocketing into the air, he shook his head and chomped the hook. Next, he tail-walked across the surface like a marlin, before splashing down and dashing up-current. Now turning, he sped downstream on a nonstop run that made my reel sing. I fought for a better grip and reared back with force enough to turn a tarpon. Fearful moments followed. I held on, praying my drag and raised rod would somehow slow King's downstream charge. But this was too fresh and strong a fish. When exposed metal flashed from the reel's spool, I knew the end was near. Things had happened so...*SNAP!*

"One instant, the exhilarating fight, then...*GONE!* I slumped dejectedly and reeled in my limp leader. *What happened?* Then it came to me: *Snag Pool*. More than once a "beaten" fish had taken refuge amongst its sunken, tangled timbers. With a roll of his body or a jerk of his head, King had snapped free. For a time, he must have been too tired to realize his newfound freedom, yet somehow thankful the strain was gone. I pictured the trout sinking to the bottom, jaws and gills working to regain its breath.

"Before leaving, I respectfully saluted my opponent. 'Till we meet again, Fish!' Turning, I made a silent promise: *I'LL BE BACK!*

"On my return home, I relived the recent events. I vowed that I was going to get this fish. I didn't know how or when, but I knew that he was going to be mine. I had worked too hard...come too close."

Jeff sighed sympathetically.

"Gosh, Gramps, what happened after that...have you seen him since?"

Gramps wearily shook his head as if wondering how many more seasons this venerable trout might be around. Then he continued.

"The following evening, I looked again, but there was no trace. Disappointed but not yet discouraged, I headed home. The next day brought another letdown. Weeks of searching produced nothing. As mysteriously as the fish had appeared, he had vanished. *What had happened?* Perhaps it had swum downstream with the spring floods, to be lost in the hundred-foot depths of the Upper Lake. Still, I continued my quest. The weeks turned to months. I was beginning to despair. *Why wouldn't the trout show himself?* I had tried the pool time and again, not believing it able to jump the falls. So I concentrated on likely spots downstream. I could not find the big brookie. My search had become an obsession that was disrupting my sleep. My normally patient wife, your grandma, was growing concerned about my distraction. Finally, there came the point when I actually gave up hope.

"Then, last month at Brown's Country Store, in walked a fisherman, wide-eyed and bedraggled. He looked so shaken, I *had* to ask what happened.

"That morning, he recalled working up Crystal Creek and coming upon a beautiful pool below a falls."

"'*Tall Pines Pool!*' I thought to myself. '*Could it be?*' I encouraged him to continue.

"The fisherman recounted changing flies when he noticed a field mouse fall into the water. As the current swept the struggling creature to center pool, he noticed a long, dark shape materialize below.

"Just as the fisherman jerked his head to swat a fly, the center of the pool exploded with spray. By the time he refocused, nothing remained but concentric rings. Excitedly, he searched the water before tearing back to town with the tale of something dwelling in Tall Pines Pool that splashed fishermen while swallowing field mice.

"You can imagine, Jeff, this story was greeted with laughter and disbelief.

"'Probably an otter,' someone shrugged. Still, something in the man's face reminded me of my first encounter with King. Before leaving the store, I asked him to keep things quiet. A lot of good that did!

"The next morning, a half dozen trophy seekers, armed with heavy gear and great expectations, set upon the Preserve. They raced up to Tall Pines

Pool and crisscrossed it with every size and color counterfeit imaginable. But they got nothing for their trouble. One by one, they returned to their homes to join those who believed the commotion had been caused by an otter. Finally, the rumor died, until only I believed. *But where was the trout?*"

"Gramps, have you tried for him since?" asked Jeff.

"No, but it's been over a month now—time enough for the ol' boy to have cooled off. I've been itching to look some more." Gramps's determined look melted into a smile. "Of course, I wanted to wait for your expert assistance!"

Sensing Jeff about to prolong the conversation, his grandfather interrupted.

"Uh, uh, that's enough, slugger! Tomorrow's a big day, so do yourself a favor and get some shut-eye."

Following Gramps's exciting account, *how was he to sleep?* Jeff bid his grandfather "goodnight" and reluctantly withdrew to the lean-to. Snuggled within his sleeping bag atop a fragrant bed of balsam, he gazed into the star-filled heavens. Soon, he was fast asleep.

CHAPTER 9

DAY 2:

MORNING AT TREE TOP LODGE;
WINDY POINT

In the dark hours of early morning, Jeff awoke to a loon's haunting call. He loved the sound, for it came from a creature of the wilderness. He had first heard its lonesome cry in Maine; it was a sound he would never forget.

"Rise and shine!" Gramps tugged playfully at his grandson's sleeping bag.

Today was the day! Jeff sat up and briskly rubbed himself to increase blood flow. He reached for his clothes and quickly dressed. Within minutes, he was standing before the fire, enjoying its warmth while sipping hot chocolate. After finishing a refill, he grasped the camp ax and split a fire log in two. He lay the splits atop the stirred coals and blew until they burst into flame. The early morning chill was offset by the welcome increase of heat. It

47

seemed only hours since he'd gone to bed, but the fresh air and anticipation of the upcoming events contributed to his feeling rested and raring to go.

The camp glittered in morning frost. Etched in its white dusting were numerous spoor marking the nocturnal wanderings of rabbit, squirrel, and raccoon.

Jeff spied a convergence of tracks at the base of a large beech tree. Thirty feet up its trunk, two young raccoons peered out from an old cavity.

Jeff admired these masked marauders for their intelligence and the nimble way they manipulated their paws like tiny human hands. A raccoon's compact body, sharp teeth, and claws allowed it to stage a formidable defense if provoked. When pursued by a dog in water, they had been known to overpower their tormentor.

At Jeff's summer camp, a large male had once been confined in a steel cage whose hinged door was weighted and wired at the top. The next morning, this raccoon was nowhere to be found, having escaped like Houdini from its "escape-proof" confines.

"Breakfast is about ready!"

The smell of bacon filled the air. Jeff approached the fire and stared at thick slices sizzling in the frying pan. Alongside was a stack of buttered pancakes covered with real maple syrup. Jeff recalled fall in Vermont, cruising through lofty "tunnels" of golden sugar maples affixed with collecting buckets. *Because weather fluctuations altered sap density, up to eighty gallons of tree sap had to be simmered down to make a single gallon of condensed syrup.*

After breakfast, Jeff entered the kitchen woodshed and retrieved firewood for the cook stove. As he was delivering an armful to his grandmother, he heard a rustling outside. Only yards away, a glassy-eyed doe was looking at him through an opened window.

"Wow, look at that! She sure is a beauty!"

Grandma whispered, "Been coming around here for the past two seasons. Almost like a pet, she is, but still pretty wild. Look closely and maybe you can find her fawn."

Methodically, Jeff scanned the area until his perseverance was rewarded, discovering white spots against a russet background. The fawn's motionless, low-lying posture, dappled markings, and lack of scent helped protect it from predators.

After enjoying this latest adventure, Jeff joined his grandfather on the front porch, preparing for the day's fishing. Gramps was assembling his seven-foot sectional fly rod. The "Orvis" trademark identified it as a precision piece esteemed by many fishermen. Constructed from eight strands of bamboo, the rod was pressure-bonded to form a hexagonal shaft that was considered without peer for beauty and function. Jeff noted its thinness.

"Isn't that a little light for the fish we're going after?"

"Appearances can be deceiving. With the right drag setting and proper handling, this little buggy whip can wear down a pretty hefty fish. Hopefully, you'll see for yourself!"

Jeff nodded, then asked, "Where's a good place to dig for worms?"

"Try near the base of the cabin."

"Thanks, see you in a few!"

Jeff descended the stairway. He fetched a shovel from the tool shed, then looked around until he spotted an area where the soil looked moist and loamy. Driving his shovel in and overturning it, he knelt down, plucked several lively earthworms, and dropped them into a dirt-filled can. Two shovelfuls yielded nine plump worms. One of these squirming morsels trailing a flashing spinner was an irresistible combination.

Gramps descended the stairs.

"How'd you make out?"

"Fine, the soil's full of worms."

"That's because I dump my coffee grounds at that spot; worms thrive on them."

"Where are we fishing today?"

"Think we'll try the Cove for starters."

As the name implied, Fish Cove was a renowned "hot spot," offering action from several species of game fish. Here, the cool spring water of Crystal Creek mixed with the sun-warmed shallows of the Upper Lake. The Cove's drop-offs teemed with life while providing ideal cover for pickerel, smallmouth bass, and an occasional trout.

With tackle in hand, the two adventurers descended to the lake. Its surface was dimpled by feeding fish. A water snake glided by, making good time as it swam toward its morning sunning spot. Its neck was arched above water as it steadily "S'd" along. Reaching shore, it slithered up through the thorny branches of an overhanging bush to intertwine and bask with another of its kind.

A bullfrog bellowed. Its sonorous calling evoked pleasant memories of falling asleep to conversing frogs during camping trips. The chorus ranged from the booming bass of bullfrogs to the high, clear chirps of the spring peepers. The bigger frogs possessed voracious appetites—ingesting crayfish, snakes, frogs, even fishing lures.

Jeff never forgot his surprise when, grasping a large bullfrog, it had emitted a sustained high-pitched whine. *Such a sound would surely scare off most predators!*

Jeff chose a suitable paddle, then loaded his gear into the center of the canoe for the best weight distribution. Climbing into the bow section, he sat down and waited.

"Ready?"

The boy nodded.

Gramps pushed off and soon their paddles swung in unison. As the canoe accelerated, sunlight breaking through the trees created a pleasant strobe effect. They moved into open water and glided toward a spur of land known as Windy Point.

"Stroke...stroke...stroke!" Each thrust made the canoe surge forward, bow wave gurgling. Craggy pines and lake bottom stones passed by at a clip. They were making good time. Already they had reached their first marker and were now bearing down on a huge pine tree that dominated Windy Point. With no slackening of pace, they strove toward the landmark.

"Switch."

Paddles swung to opposite sides as back and shoulder muscles labored. Despite growing fatigue, the exercise felt good.

Suddenly Gramps pointed to a dark speck out at mid lake. First thought to be a floating log, closer examination revealed the speck to be in motion.

Surprise! A young black bear was doggy-paddling to the opposite shore.

Without hesitation, Gramps grabbed his paddle and shouted, "Let's go!"

Jeff looked incredulous.

"Go after a bear?"

Gramps grinned, "We're not going to lasso or ride it—just get a closer look."

In synchronized motion, the two bore down on their paddles until they were maintaining maximum speed. There was something special about moving at such a pace—feeling your craft respond to your strokes, smelling the breeze in your face, and hearing the pronounced thumping of your heart.

When the paddlers drew alongside the bear, it snorted in alarm. They enjoyed escorting it toward shore; before gaining foothold, it humorously splashed and floundered. Without pause for a body shake, it then dashed into the woods. Snapping undergrowth marked its retreat until silence ruled again.

"You won't be seeing *him* for quite some time!" Gramps chuckled, patting Jeff's knee.

After savoring their excitement, they turned toward Windy Point. On the far side was Fish Cove, its promising waters beckoning.

Guarding the cove's entrance, a lone pine towered like a huge clipper ship's mast. They headed for it and beached on a reed-covered sandbar.

Jeff crossed the pebble-strewn shore and approached the pine. He embraced its six-foot breadth and gazed seventy-five feet up to where its first burly limbs extended over the sparkling lake. Higher still was a gnarled concentration of limbs and branches, some dead and weathered, most laden with green needles. One hundred and fifty feet up, a fresh breeze filled the uppermost "sails" and played a soft, distant tune as if trying to share some secret from the tree's venerable past. The largest survivor of the nineteenth-century logging days, the pine was spared as a seed tree to resupply the denuded area with seedlings, ensuring future harvests for use in homes, ships, and the railroad. For centuries it stood sentinel, a living monument of its lakeside domain.

Jeff ran his hands along the fibrous bark sheathing the trunk in bold, distinctive plates. Supporting the massive tree, a surrounding network of serpentine roots extended underground beyond the outermost limbs. High aloft on a bare branch, an osprey raised itself and unfolded its checkered black and white wings. Ruffling its feathers, it cocked its head and directed its keen gaze downward. Evolution had enabled the fish hawk to spot a small fish from hundreds of feet above. Furthermore, the bird was able to overcome the optical illusion of light refracting through choppy, sun-glared water. By aiming at "open" water next to where the fish appeared, the bird often hit its mark.

The hawk extended the feathered planes of its wings and pushed off. A rising thermal lifted the bird skyward. Ascending ever higher, it leisurely circled a half-dozen times. Suddenly, it pressed its wings to its body and plummeted toward the lake. Hitting the water feet first, it disappeared in an explosion of spray. Moments later, it emerged like an overloaded cargo plane, its flapping wings struggling to gain enough speed for lift off. But the fish clutched in its raspy talons was too heavy; after several exhausting attempts, the fish hawk was forced to drop its unwieldy prize.

It was not long, however, before the hungry bird's perseverance was rewarded by a seven-inch catch of flopping silver. Flying just above the lake surface, the osprey gained speed until, with a triumphant screech, it ascended to its favorite perch atop the pine. There, it began to dine.

Jeff had heard about a thrilling midair confrontation between an osprey and a bald eagle; after bullying the smaller hawk into releasing its catch, the eagle had swooped down and acrobatically snatched the falling fish before it hit water.

Jeff's reminiscence ended with Gramps' call: "Hop in, this ship's leaving."

However, when the boy spotted the weathered ruins of a nineteenth-century sawmill, he begged for a closer look. It was fun exploring among wildflowers and discovering artifacts—iron wheels, spikes, and chains from a bygone age.

Jutting out into the bay were the remains of dock pilings. Here was a favorite lurking place for smallmouth bass—scrappy fighters whose fins bristled and red eyes glared when landed.

Jeff looked forward to the upcoming fishing.

CHAPTER 10

FISHING AT FISH COVE

Abandoning the pleasurable adventures of Windy Point, they drifted into the still waters of Fish Cove. The young fisherman was impressed by its potential. Miniature forests of aquatic vegetation bordered a deepwater channel extending up Crystal Creek. Fishing was especially good along its weedy embankments, where game fish lay to ambush smaller fish cruising the channel.

While preparing his tackle, Jeff paused to admire the master fisherman at work. Gramps knowingly gripped the rod in his right hand and alternately brought his casting arm back and forth in smooth, sweeping motions. While doing so, he steadily fed out line with his left hand to increase the distance of the cast. The moment the back-cast "loaded" his rod, he swept his arm toward his target, causing the flexed rod to spring forward and shoot out an impressive length of line. Traveling in a low, graceful arc, his fly settled atop the water like a natural insect.

Gramps teased it several minutes before lifting up line and false-casting again. Swish…swishh…swishhh… Following another forward sweep of his forearm, the tapered line sailed across the calm lake.

As Gramps retrieved, he methodically drew lengths of line through the ferrules, causing his fly to "swim" with lifelike motion. When no strike occurred, Gramps raised his arm, flicked his wrist and lifted the remaining line off the water. Swish…swishh…swishhh…back and forth, this time aiming at a half-submerged tree stump bordering a deeper drop-off. He waited until the concentric circles died away, then twitched his rod. The fly trembled enticingly.

"If there's a fish below, you can bet it's heard the dinner gong! Sometimes you'll get a strike before your lure hits water…it's also exciting trying to coax 'em into action."

As Gramps worked his lure, he described the function of a fish's lateral line.

"Sound and motion travel much better through water than air; when their waves hit a fish's nerve endings, it senses food or danger."

SP-PLASH! A big bronze fish rocketed skyward and landed headfirst. Engulfing the bait, it felt the hook and shot off on a wrist-wrenching run that made Gramps' reel sing.

"Wee-owhh—look at 'im go! What is it?"

"Smallmouth, and a big one to boot!"

Jeff followed the action as his grandfather's rod jerked downward in response to the bass's short, powerful runs. The smallmouth in these cold northern waters were noted for their fighting ability. This brute proved no exception as it sped toward the sanctuary of its root-guarded home. In an instant, it was gone.

"Blasted!" Gramps looked at his limp line, then grew excited. "Did you *see* him, Jeff?!"

The boy nodded, recalling the glistening breadth of its gold-green sides striped with black vertical bars.

"How big, Gramps?"

"Three and a half, maybe four pounds—a nice one for sure!" The fisherman nodded toward the stump. "He'll be down a while…We'll try for him later," adding that, like many fish, smallmouths feed over a wide area but have preferred hangouts.

Gramps broke off several feet of line before retying.

"This gets rid of unseen frays that weaken the line." He winked at Jeff. "Looks like you're still in the running for first fish! Grab your paddle and let's see if we can stir up some action in those lily pads over there."

With quiet dips of their paddles, the fishermen drifted near a promising looking concentration of pads.

"See that open water in the middle of those lilies?" Gramps asked while casting. After his bug landed atop a bordering pad, he packed and lit his pipe and took a contented draw.

"This'll give anything down there time to think about what it wants to do."

With a casual flip, he hopped the bug into the lake. Water exploded as another bass somersaulted. Feeling unexpected resistance from the plug in its jaw, the smallmouth sped off, bulldozing through a forest of lily stems.

This fish was even larger than the previous one; its power, coupled with the drag from uprooted vegetation, strained Gramps's tackle.

"Whoooah-boy! No waiting for action today!" Gramps tried to lead the fish out into open water, but this bronze-back had a mind of its own. Intent on causing a commotion, it flopped, arched, and splashed over an ever-enlarging area. Shallow water and pressure from Gramps' rod forced the bass into the spray-filled air. Falling like stone, it pumped the rod downward as it bore into dense vegetation. Then it tore loose and sped around the canoe's bow with pond weed trailing its quivering body. It tried to reenter the lilies, but Gramps, anticipating its intent, countered with stiff rod pressure. Meanwhile, he directed his partner to maneuver the boat to a more advantageous playing position.

After several more thrilling jumps, the bass finally succumbed to the relentless pressure. Winded and weary, the fish was skated over the tops of lilies and drawn toward the boat's side.

"I'm going to lead him in slowly so he doesn't spook. Wait until I ease him over the net before you make your move, OK?"

"Gotcha."

"Here he comes."

With its broad hump protruding above the water, the smallmouth was drawn even closer.

"Steady...S T E A D Y ! Don't stab at him, boy!"

Too weak to evade the inevitable, the bass slipped over the mesh. With a quick uplift, Jeff swung the laden net into the canoe. The entangled fish began a staccato barrage of tail-smacking against the aluminum bottom.

"He's in the boat, he's in the boat—we got 'im!"

Jeff leaned over for a closer look. "Come see! He's BEAUTIFUL!"

"That he is," Gramps acknowledged, as both admired the full-bodied fish, powerfully built with a broad back and fins bristling in seeming defiance. Its red eye glared up at the unfamiliar surroundings.

"Want to keep him?" Gramps kidded as he handed his companion the stringer.

Just as the boy was about to painlessly insert its point through the fish's lips, the bass raised its spiny dorsal and, with a spasmodic flip, flopped from Jeff's grip to the canoe floor. Before descending hands could secure its slippery bulk, it threw the lure and jack-knifed out of the boat. Momentarily, it lay on its side within reach of the shocked fishermen. Then it righted itself and, with a *swish* of its tail, was gone.

"We HAD him! He was OURS!" Jeff groaned.

Gramps shook his head but put a reassuring arm around his flustered grandson. "Can't say this is the first fish that has gotten away, but our luck can only get better. Right, sport?"

Jeff's weak smile betrayed his disappointment as he slumped down.

Twenty minutes passed uneventfully. Suddenly, Jeff stood and pointed.

"What's up?" Gramps asked.

"Over there!"

The elder man sighted down his grandson's extended arm.

"Do you see it?"

"Ah, yes—nice rise!"

The dimpling water looked like that made by a feeding trout. The fishermen headed closer. Soon, concentric rings reappeared.

"There he goes again! What's he eating?"

"Probably caddisfly nymphs hatching this time of year."

Jeff inquired whether their talking would scare the fish.

"Not usually, if you keep it low. It's the amplified noise from boat-banging that really causes 'em to scatter!"

Still, a low quiet approach was less likely to spook a wary fish in clear water.

When they neared casting range, the fishermen let the canoe's momentum carry them in. Gurgling water diminished as the canoe drifted to a stop.

Gramps leaned over and handed Jeff a fly.

"Here, see what you can do with this."

While his grandfather back-paddled for a broadside cast, the boy studied the bristly hand-tied creation.

Gramps spoke again; "Doesn't look like much, but trout seem to like 'em. Same pattern fooled my four-pounder back at camp."

"Where did you get it?"

When Gramps pointed ahead, the younger fisherman reflexively reached for his rod and began false-casting. Moving his right hand back and forth, he played out line with his left hand. When one back-cast grazed water, Gramps encouraged his grandson to keep casting.

"Relax and your timing will come."

Successive casts became easier.

"A few more feet…that's it!"

To Jeff's surprise, nearly thirty feet of line arched across the water. When the fly alighted several yards ahead of the foraging fish, Gramps elbowed his grandson and whispered, "Perfect…and you didn't spook him! Now start bumping it along the lake bottom…not too much…*that's* better!"

By periodically twitching the rod, Jeff imparted a lifelike crawl to the caddisfly.

Suddenly, the fish flashed across the bottom, struck the bait, and went airborne.

"Rainbow trout! First I've seen in a while. It's a good one, too!"

Jeff was thrilled. Meanwhile, the fish fought a spirited battle befitting its species, leaping and arching through showers of spray.

"Play 'im carefully, son. He's a special catch if you can land him. Lower your rod when he jumps…keep tension and take up slack when you can."

The trout jumped again, its colorful body framed against blue sky. Eventually, it tired. Jeff began leading it over to his grandfather's half-submerged landing net.

Gramps coaxed, "Come on, bring him in. A little closer… THAT'S IT!"

Jeff slid the trout atop the motionless mesh; Gramps quickly lifted and swung the laden net toward his grandson.

"HE'S ALL YOURS!" he beamed proudly.

The boy scrambled over and gazed down at the speckled foot-long fish. Sandwiched between its green back and white belly was a rose-pink band; *it was easy to see how the rainbow had earned its name!*

Jeff questioned destroying such a beauty, but when he recalled enjoying crisp, tender trout, his face brightened.

"Tastes as good as it looks! We'll have it for breakfast tomorrow."

Gramps handed his grandson a stringer. "Put the cord through the lips so it can breathe better."

This done, Jeff lowered the trout overboard and watched it fin beneath the drifting boat.

CHAPTER 11

THE SEARCH FOR "KING" CONTINUES

It was time to search for the Tall Pines trout. Picking up their strokes and feeling optimistic from their morning success, the fishermen headed toward Crystal Creek. They entered its wide backwaters and meandered upstream. Jeff peered through transparent water at passing beds of undulating river grass.

Rounding a bend, they surprised a family of mergansers. Wing-flapping and squawking erupted as the panicked fish ducks sprinted across the water attempting to lift off; once airborne, they flew a short way upstream and splashed down.

When the canoe re-approached the paddling birds, the episode was repeated. After several takeoffs and landings, the agitated group circled past and hurried downstream.

Jeff chuckled, "I was beginning to wonder if they'd *ever* catch on!"

The stream's darkening outer curves indicated increased depth and slowed current. Now the adventurers made good time cruising past daisy-filled meadows shimmering with rustling aspens. Proceeding further, they passed shady overhangs of moss-laden pines; several times, their canoe drifted beneath archways formed by trees converging from opposite banks. With muffled strokes, they paddled on. The current grew more pronounced as paper and yellow birch shared steepening hillsides with white pine and fir. Rounding a sand-bordered bend, they glided up through a long slick of dark water.

"Snag Pool ahead!"

Fifty yards upstream, the creek rounded an abrupt bend and flowed into a mass of sun-bleached driftwood. Looking from afar like a low, gleaming iceberg, the pile of weathered tree trunks and debris had been swept down during high water to become inextricably lodged at Snag Pool. Over years, the diverted current had carved a deep hole beneath the timbers, creating an ideal haven for trout.

As a boy, Gramps had trod barefoot atop the timbers and lowered worms through the sun-shafted depths. Invariably, a colorful brookie would strike, and following a short, lively tussle, the flopping eight- to ten-inch fish would be lifted and deposited in a fern-lined creel. A quick toss, a soft "ker-plunk," and another tugging trout would be on—a pleasant experience repeated two or three times before the remaining population grew too wary.

Before the bend, Gramps motioned Jeff to beach the canoe. They clambered to the top of a steep embankment and picked their way along an overgrown path overlooking the log jam. As he approached the bend, Jeff studied the pool and grew excited. *What a paradise for fish, and a nightmare for fishermen!*

On the near, deep side, the slowed current swirled lazily through a maze of tangled timbers. *There was no doubt its shaded depths harbored trout!* The trick was in getting them out. With smaller fish, a short line and quick lift was all that was needed, but when an occasional twelve-incher was hooked, the problems and excitement compounded.

After baiting his spinner with a worm, Jeff slid down onto an old, solid section of the log jam. Proceeding outward, he gingerly situated himself on a tree trunk extending over the deepest section of the pool. He let his flashing spinner flutter to the bottom, then began jigging it with a teasing up-and-down motion. He anticipated a rushing brookie, but no strike occurred.

After several repetitions, Jeff looked at Gramps.

The latter offered some advice; "Try over there. There's a sunken log lying near the bottom that usually holds a fish or two."

Jeff crept over and lowered his lure between two timbers. After watching its uneven descent, he retrieved his untouched offering. A few minutes later, Gramps motioned Jeff to another vantage point. Still there was no action.

"Where'd they all go?"

"Beats me!" Gramps shrugged, looking perplexed.

"What'll we do now, Grandpa?"

"Let's try a bit more."

Ten minutes later, Gramps broke the awkward silence.

"Let's walk upstream and see what we can find."

They collected their gear and followed the stream-side path, musing over the curious and disturbing lack of strikes at Snag Pool. The two plowed through more undergrowth before rejoining the trail. A quarter-mile upstream, the waist-deep stream glided glass-smooth over sand and undulating elodea.

Gramps spoke excitedly, "This is where I first discovered King. As large and colorful as he was, he was camouflaged on the bottom. If it hadn't been for his rise, I'd've surely passed him by!"

In spite of a careful search, the fishermen saw only the fleeting shadow of one small trout.

"No cause for alarm," Gramps explained. Increased mid-morning visibility prompted fish to lay low, making them less vulnerable to predators. During a hatch, however, fish sometimes throw caution aside.

"I've seen this stretch boiling with trout—so many you wonder where they all came from! More'n once a buddy or I would be in the thick of a hatch, pulling 'em in until our arms were sore, while the other fisherman was around the bend getting skunked and wondering where the fish had gone. By the time we rejoined, both the hatch and the fishing would have stopped.

"Equally frustrating was the time I stood within spittin' distance of a big brown trout so intent on slurping flies that it seemed unaware of my presence. Wouldn't you know I had just lost my last fly. But that's fishing!"

The two adventurers walked along the fern-bordered path, listening to the stream. In time, they heard a perceptible increase in its flow. *Rapids ahead!* Varied currents, pockets and obstructions challenged canoeists and fishermen.

Foaming fingers of white water splashed between boulders; in the clear eddies, Jeff searched for trout.

They made a gradual ascent to the head of the rapids. Beyond a sandbar, a ten-foot waterfall splashed into a swirling, emerald pool.

Shaded by ancient evergreens and encircled by mossy monoliths, it was the most beautiful place the boy had ever seen. *TALL PINES POOL!* Jeff eagerly surveyed the mountain oasis, kept naturally air-conditioned by the falls. The surrounding walls resonated as mist drifted about the spray-dampened rocks. He climbed upon a massive sixty-foot-long boulder bordering the far side of the deep, spacious pool. From here, he caught the reflective sheen of water spilling off the elevated overhang. Below the falls, a torrent of bubbles swept downstream to rise and disappear in the slow-churning depths of center pool.

"Guess how deep?" Gramps asked.

"Six feet."

"Twice that!"

The water's clarity played tricks with one's depth perception. Strewn about the bottom was a wavering concentration of rocks and boulders; the current flowing over this uneven bed formed eddies and upwellings, making the pool appear somehow alive. Fifty feet downstream, the bottom rose steeply to shallow riffles before exiting into rapids below.

Somewhere within this gem-like pool might dwell that treasure of a Trout!

Gramps tied a bright-colored fly to his leader.

"What's that?"

"It's called a Parmachene Belle. Brookies really go for 'em."

The younger fisherman tied on his spinner, then tested his knot for slippage.

"'Bout time you started fishing!" Gramps gave a teasing wink as he directed his grandson's attention to center pool. "If the old boy's still here, he's hungry and waiting. You try first."

Jeff hopped two boulders, slid down a third, and crept to the water's edge. Crouching low, he un-clicked the bail and cast. With a dull chink, the worm-baited spinner bounced off a boulder and dropped into the swift water. Instantly, the undertow pulled it deep.

The fisherman kept a tight line while the revolving spinner flashed enticingly. When the lure completed its downstream drift, he retrieved and cast again.

As the spinner bumped and fluttered over the bottom rocks, Jeff thought how this presentation lost lures but caught more fish lying in the slower, more protected water nearest the bottom. He followed each retrieval, thrilling at the thought of the big fish rushing his lure. But nothing materialized.

Gramps spoke: "Sometimes it takes time to persuade 'em. Once I cast twenty-two times over one Atlantic salmon before he finally struck. The important thing is to stick with it and don't lose your concentration. Just one mistake can put a good fish down."

Jeff stared at his rod, then at his grandfather.

"Do you think he's still in here?"

"Maybe."

Tight-lipped, the boy tossed his spinner to a prime holding area where the main current converged with a slow-moving eddy. After reeling in, he cast again and yet again, until he trudged back to his frowning grandfather.

Gramps squinted into the afternoon sun. "Wherever that fellow is, he's sure playing hard to get. Maybe it's not his mealtime yet."

He put a reassuring arm around his grandson.

"We've got the rest of the week—if he's still around, there's a good bet we'll find him."

Such a prophecy felt reassuring coming from the head fishing guide of the Ausable Preserve.

Gramps walked to the pool's edge.

"Let's see if this will stir him."

After several false casts, he sent his fly across pool and began stripping line and jerking the streamer like a live, darting minnow. Still no fish appeared.

Where WAS the trout? Had it succumbed to old age? The unknown was often hardest to deal with.

By now, the most likely hangouts had been tried, but Gramps knew other spots able to accommodate this fish. *With luck, they might still drag a lure before its broad, mossy snout.*

"Let's try beneath the falls."

Seeing Jeff's surprised look, Gramps explained, "Some fish live years hidden in water pockets passed by most fishermen. With no fishing pressure, they can grow to impressive size."

Jeff shrugged and lobbed a short cast into the froth.

Within seconds, the current swept his lure well downstream.

"What now?"

"Try again."

Following a third retrieval, Gramps recommended they head back and finish setting up camp.

"That's enough today…We'll try again tomorrow."

Jeff's grandfather empathized with his grandson's obvious disappointment.

"We gave it our best, didn't we? Tomorrow we'll put our heads together and see if we can turn our luck."

While paddling home, Jeff reviewed the day's events. *How strange: two top fishing holes seemingly without fish.* One possible explanation: *little fish become scarce where bigger fish reside.*

The trout's diet was considered. Lures and flies might still fool this wary brookie, but its age and size attested to its selective feeding habits. Having seen its share of artificials, this seasoned veteran no doubt desired something large and live—a fish's equivalent of a T-bone steak.

Jeff imagined King masterfully camouflaged on the stony bottom. Sensing faint vibrations with its lateral line, the aroused fish would rush out and clamp down on an unsuspecting minnow, then resume its original lie for a leisurely head-first gulp. After resting, it would again rise like a submarine to glide through the dappled depths, the undisputed monarch of its domain.

71

Ever watchful for scattering bait fish, it daily exercised its instinctive ritual of eating, resting and self-preservation. To fool and land this trout would be an achievement well beyond "beginners' luck." Jeff weighed his chances and realized this fish was still only as close as his dreams.

CHAPTER 12

DAY 3:

JEFF ON HIS OWN

The next morning, Gramps announced he would be guiding a fishing client. Although Jeff enjoyed his grandfather's company, the prospect of being on his own was appealing. Intent on maximizing his time, he packed lunch, grabbed his fishing gear, and descended to the dock. Hurrying to the minnow trap, he hoisted its meshed cage.

Surprise! A young catfish flopped about inside. Jeff initially thought the bait too large, but remembered that big fish like big meals. Once he had caught a perch on a musky lure; another time, he found a bass suffocated on a sunfish. *The catfish should make an irresistible offering.*

Eager to test his big-bait/big-fish theory, he set off to find King. *Snag Pool would be a good place for starters.* Quick, powerful strokes caused his light craft to skim past regiments of high-spired trees. Jeff listened to water gurgling alongside and the faint hissing of bow bubbles bursting. He was relishing his independence.

A distant frog croaked. *It was amazing how audible the sound was, having traveled across the lake.*

He was approaching Windy Point, its towering pine dominating the horizon. As he passed beneath its dizzying height, the only sounds heard were his beating heart, heavy breathing, and the music of the cruising canoe. Golden light poured over the awakening lowlands, warming the air. Jeff's world was calm. He was at peace with himself.

He heard faint honking. Turning, he saw the horizon darkened by hundreds of flying birds; a massive migration of Canadian geese was making its annual return from southern feeding grounds. Unending formations etched the skyline, their patterns constantly changing. In the distance, the slow-moving mass looked like a huge swarm of bees.

As they approached, the air began to reverberate with their noisy, nonstop chorus. Now the first formation swept majestically overhead, spanning the sky in a close-strung "V" of some fifty geese. These were followed by wave after wave, each filling the air with whistling wings and musical honking.

For ten full minutes, Jeff marveled at the spectacle—passing flocks replaced by seemingly inexhaustible numbers of newcomers. Instinctively disciplined, they swiftly propelled their streamlined bodies through the swirling sky with rapid down-sweeps of their semi-stiff wings.

Jeff was thrilled to have witnessed this rare event; after the last configuration grew small, he savored the experience while taking up his paddle.

Just below Snag Pool, Jeff beached the canoe with a soft thud on mashed grass. He climbed up the embankment and quietly lowered himself onto the log jam. He opened the bait bucket, grasped the catfish, and slipped a hook through its fleshy lips. Tossing it onto the foam-flecked surface, he waited nervously as it dove for the bottom.

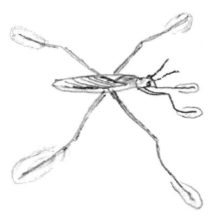

After five minutes, Jeff passed time watching water striders skittering about the stream. The wide and equalized stance of these stick-like insects enabled them to stay afloat without breaking the surface tension of the water. *Why weren't these insects gobbled by fish?* Certain plants and animals possess varied defense mechanisms; *maybe water striders tasted bad.*

Jeff reeled in and cast to where a mossy log slanted deep into the pool. After several minutes of feeling the catfish exploring the bottom, he lay back, propped the rod on his knees, and nibbled on a peanut butter and jelly sandwich.

Suddenly, the rod dipped, then straightened. Rushing with adrenalin, Jeff jumped up, grabbed hold, and felt his bait's movements telegraphing through the line. *It was tugging as if TRYING TO ESCAPE!*

Again, the rod plunged in response to a steady, powerful pull… seconds later, the leader snapped and the rod straightened.

It could only be…HAD to be…The TROUT!

———————— · ————————

"GRA-A-AMPS!" Jeff rushed into the cabin.

"Whoa, Jeffey-boy, what is it, lad, what is it?"

In a torrent of words, the young fisherman described how his catfish had been grabbed by something in Snag Pool.

As the boy's tale unfolded, Gramps's grin widened. *The Monarch had been found at last.* Yet an aching reality was evident: to maneuver this monster up through the maze of timbers seemed an impossible feat.

"If he's in Snag, we have a problem," Gramps affirmed, shaking his head. As long as the fish remained entrenched within its root-entwined fortress, it could never be landed. Still, they were excited about the discovery and the possibility of playing the fish, if only briefly.

CHAPTER 13

DAY 4: TIME IS RUNNING OUT;

A WELCOME DIVERSION—
THE CLIMB UP LOOKOUT MOUNTAIN

By the fourth day, Jeff felt an increased sense of urgency. Arriving with Gramps at Snag Pool, he baited his hook and plopped it into the slow-churning current. For a time, he felt his minnow swimming freely. Soon, increased tremors told him the Trout was near. Moments later, Jeff felt its pronounced tug.

"What s-should I do," Jeff stammered, "What should I do?"

"Give him line. Let him run."

Jeff followed his grandfather's instructions by clicking open the reel's bail and allowing line to unravel. With the bait clamped in its jaws, the trout swam leisurely. Jeff's hands sweat as the moments lengthened. Soon the fish began to slow; finally, it stopped.

"WHAT NOW?"

"Stay with him. He'll be starting up again." Gramps predicted the trout would repeat this tactic before pausing to turn the minnow headfirst for a final gulp.

"Until then you just have to sweat it out!"

How much longer must he wait? How much longer COULD he wait? It was HARD not knowing when to strike! If he pulled up too early or too late, he was sure to lose the fish.

Jeff's eyes begged for the go-ahead that never seemed to come. Then the line became still.

Could the fish be preparing to swallow? Excitedly, Jeff reared back and felt his rod strain against solid weight…an instant later, it sprang straight as his bait shot into the air.

D A R N! *He had struck too soon—pulled the bait right out of the trout's mouth!*

The moment left the two fishermen gasping. Numbed with disappointment, Jeff sat down. *HE SHOULD HAVE WAITED FOR GRAMPS'S SIGNAL!*

Jeff's grandfather came over and put a reassuring arm around the boy's shoulder.

He added a positive thought: "We've got 'im interested, that's for sure."

"What now?"

"He's spooked. We'll rest him until tomorrow. Nothing more we can do."

After allowing Jeff time to process his disappointment, Gramps tried diverting his grandson's attention. He pointed upstream to a huge mountain dominating the skyline.

"How would you like to climb the third highest peak in New York?"

Jeff loved climbing everything from ropes to rocks to trees. Though still reeling from the recent encounter, he welcomed Gramps's offer.

"Sounds good to me. When?"

"How about right now?"

"What's its elevation?"

"About three thousand feet higher than we're standing."

78

Jeff looked at his watch and computed the mountain's size with the amount of daylight remaining.

"Will we have time?

Gramps grinned. "If we sleep on the mountain, yes." He described a lean-to he and Jeff's great-grandfather had built nearly fifty years ago. "Let's head back to camp and pack some gear."

With the aid of the current, the adventurers enjoyed a speedy return. Upon entering Fish Cove, however, foamy breakers slowed their passage.

"Where'd all this wind come from?"

"Bit different from this morning, huh, lad?"

"I see what you mean about mountain weather!"

Gramps observed the passing clouds and spoke optimistically, "Looks like another temporary front."

The canoe plowed through waves that smacked its pitching bow and sent up soaking spray. Jeff shot Gramps a relieved look, acknowledging that their struggle would be comparatively short-lived. After laboring a mile, they rounded Camp Point. Within minutes, they had docked and were trudging up to inform Ma Forster of their plan.

When climbing the stairs, Jeff noticed a light-colored timber running the base length of the cabin. Curiosity aroused, he inquired how it could have been placed under such an immensely heavy structure.

Gramps solved the mystery.

"Son, the operation is performed much the same way you change a tire, although you use much heavier equipment. By turning large screw jacks, one end of the building was raised until supporting blocks could be inserted. The procedure was repeated at the opposite end, until there was clearance enough to remove the rotted timber and roll under a fresh new one. All that remained was a lowering of the jacks, and there you have it."

Jeff's grandmother greeted them on the porch. "What are you two gents up to? Back a bit early, aren't you?"

"Just making a pit-stop and seeing if you'd like to join us for some sailing. There's a good blow out there."

Ma Forster smiled before declining. "Three's a crowd and besides, I have things to do. You two go have fun!"

"Thanks, we will!"

When all was packed, they bade Ma Forster goodbye and headed to the dock for reloading. Jeff gave his grandfather a puzzled look.

"What's this about sailing—I don't see a sailboat?"

Gramps pointed at the canoe, then produced a weathered pine bough, straight and sturdy.

"See if you can find a second like it."

Within minutes, Jeff returned.

"That'll do nicely."

The boy assisted in lashing the crossed poles together to form a crude mast. This was secured with taut cord to the canoe's bow, stern, and side gunwales. Several ponchos stretched between the mast served as their sail.

Immediately the wind found and bellowed the plastic, and the craft began to move.

"Wheee-oh! Here we go-o-o!"

Riding the waves was like being on a mini-roller coaster. Overtaking crest after crest, they would surge up, break through, and slide down their moving slopes.

Rounding Windy Point in good time, they entered Fish Cove, where they dismantled their rigging and took to their paddles.

"Hey, I'm spoiled!" Jeff teased as he initiated a few playful strokes.

The increased current of Crystal Creek made Jeff further appreciate the luxury of their sailing experience. Invigorated, they forged up the lower bends and straightaways. When they glided through Snag Pool, Jeff stared longingly into its blackened depths. Gramps sensed his grandson's thoughts.

"We'll stop and try for him tomorrow on the way home."

The fish remained on the boy's mind until he heard the rushing water below Tall Pines Pool.

"Time to portage."

They beached at the foot of the rapids.

"It's a short carry, so we'll leave everything aboard."

In unison, the two voyagers hefted the loaded canoe onto their shoulders. When their burden was balanced, they began the steeply winding ascent up and around the falls. Above its brink, they slid the canoe into a glassy run and re-embarked.

Their upstream passage meandered past forested mountains. Again they beached and walked the canoe up through a steep-walled gorge. After navigating one hundred yards of foam and rocks, they waded across shallow riffles to enter the haunting and beautiful arena of Tall Pines Pool.

While Gramps tethered the canoe, Jeff scurried up the massive pool-side boulder. Fifteen feet above the waterline, he peered down.

"See any fish?"

"Nope, not a one."

The shadowy forms of several trout could usually be spotted from Jeff's vantage point, but their absence caused no concern.

Reboarding the canoe, they paddled along scenic stretches bordered by diminishing stands of conifers.

The forest now gave way to marshland filled with alder and clump birch.

Jeff broke the silence. "Hey, look at that wall of sticks up ahead. It must be five feet high!"

A beaver dam stretched from bank to bank. Chiseled stubs of felled saplings bristled along the shorelines. Jeff sighted several stumps over a foot in diameter. Astonished, he inquired why beavers bothered with such large trees.

"For food, mainly. Such trees provide a lasting source of the beaver's favorite food—the cambium layer beneath the bark. Like most rodents, beavers have to gnaw to exercise their jaws and keep their incisor teeth from growing too long."

"Bet those trees gave some critter a real workout!"

"No doubt," Gramps affirmed.

When they reached the dam, Jeff disembarked and climbed atop the sloping structure. Curious about its sturdiness, he unsuccessfully tried dislodging some of its interwoven, mud-packed sticks.

Some dams had grown from generations of beavers, each adding on or making repairs to enlarge and deepen their backed-up pond. Alongside newer additions were older sections supporting saplings.

Jeff peered cautiously over the brink and spied a beaver making a "V" wake as it swam toward a mound of branches rising out at mid-pond.

Gramps explained that beavers could enter their homes through several underwater passageways leading to submerged food caches. Their stick and mud dome is strong enough to withstand the pawings of a hungry bear; if such digging occurred, the beaver family could easily escape through these underwater exits.

Suddenly, the beaver's tail slapped water with a loud *smack*, warning of intruders.

Gramps noted the flat leathery tail's other uses: it balances the animal when it gnaws and eats, it acts as a rudder while swimming, and it becomes a storage reservoir where fat can be converted to energy when food is scarce.

The small pond shimmered peacefully in the sun. Beneath five feet of transparent water, the bottom was strewn with sticks stripped and discarded by feeding beavers. Here and there, fertile blankets of vegetation supported a variety of aquatic life. Several trout cruised the depths in search of food. Jeff followed their unhurried passage as they periodically dimpled the surface.

A muffled "whoosh" of wings announced the arrival of a great blue heron. Swooping down and alighting in the shallows, it folded its three-foot wings and began to stalk for fish, frogs, snakes, and turtles. Supremely adapted for hunting, it inched forward a step or two and froze, looking and listening intently.

Suddenly, the bird snapped its snakelike neck down, spearing a fish with its rapier bill. Tossing its head upward, it acrobatically flipped its prey in midair and swallowed it headfirst. Jeff tracked the outsized morsel's passage down the heron's narrow throat.

He had learned birds were closer related to dinosaurs than his pet iguana. Skeptical at first, Jeff acknowledged that chickens' three-pronged scaled feet *were* more dinosaur-like than the fingered appendages of his lizard.

CHAPTER 14

CAMPING ON LOOKOUT MOUNTAIN

It was time to begin the climb. Tethering the canoe to the dam, the hikers hoisted their packs and headed toward the monolithic rise. The overgrown path quickly steepened and all but disappeared. Soon, they were forced to climb on all fours, seeking hand- and footholds wherever possible. Slowly traversing up the mountainside, they paused to regroup beneath a near-vertical incline of brittle, unstable rock. Situated atop this formidable section was a granite outcrop promising needed haven.

Climaxing a strenuous and lengthy effort, the two climbers clawed their way up onto its sun-warmed surface and gratefully collapsed. After catching their breath, they relished a candy bar and enjoyed the view.

Twenty minutes later, they resumed climbing. It helped knowing the hardest was behind them; periodically, they paused to listen to their labored breathing and mark their progress. Again, the weather was with them: sunny, with breeze enough to evaporate some perspiration. Jeff was growing thirsty.

"Darn…I forgot my canteen!"

Gramps smiled. "You're in luck. There's a spring a quarter mile ahead—water like you've never tasted!"

With new initiative, Jeff increased the pace.

In time, they came upon a proliferation of ferns. Just uphill, spring water splashed from a rock fissure and gurgled over mossy stones. Crouching on all fours, Jeff straddled the sparkling rivulet. He gratefully gulped chilled mouthfuls until his belly swelled and teeth ached. *He had heard of the purifying properties of ground filtration, and now he was enjoying its results.*

After Gramps took his turn, the rejuvenated hikers loaded up and renewed their climb.

Jeff asked, "Think we'll make the top by nightfall?"

Gramps squinted into the sun. "Should be time enough to reach tonight's campsite."

They continued upward. After another hour of heavy exertion, a heaving Gramps wiped his brow.

"Don't know about you, but I've about had it."

"How much longer before we stop?"

Jeff's grandfather pointed to a second rocky overhang well above where they were standing.

"On top is a flat area with a lean-to, a nice spot with an even nicer view!"

They climbed the steepening incline until they reached the cliff supporting the granite outcrop.

"What'll we do now?" Jeff looked stymied.

"Experts use rope, hammers, and pitons to go up, upside down, and over…we go *around!*"

Even so, the circuitous journey was exhausting. As they inched across the precipitous slope clutching whatever their tired hands could grasp, Jeff marveled at his elder companion's stamina. *It might not be Mt. Everest, but the climb was HARD!*

At last they were nearing the end of their labors…*a few more yards.* Jeff staggered up onto the elevated clearing and celebrated, pumping upraised arms.

"We made it!"

He inched over to the precipice and peered timidly into space. *Whew!* Feeling a flutter of vertigo, he retreated a few steps. *It was as if he were on an eagle's perch, with the whole world beneath him!*

After his adrenaline lessened, Jeff's oncoming fatigue prompted him to seek a level site. Padding a suitable area with moss, both climbers lay atop their unrolled sleeping bags, fast fading into well-earned rest.

———————— · ————————

Jeff awoke to a red sinking sun. Noticing the meager wood supply, he searched the mountainside and returned with arms full of dry timber.

Soon the *chop* of the ax was heard above a crackling new fire. Gramps was crouched on all fours, coaxing a tiny flame rising from birch bark shavings. Highly combustible, the oil-rich bark quickly ignited the upper layers of close-lying twigs.

"Jeff, hand me some of the smaller pieces you've got there…thanks."

After crisscrossing these with parallels of progressively thicker wood, Gramps blew steadily at the fire's base. Once the fire was self-sustaining, Gramps shared some advice.

"It's important to space your wood just right. Logs too far apart lose draft and heat; logs too close don't draft well, either."

The now-roaring campfire popped and hissed; escaping gases spiraled sparks into the sky. By the time a rose-colored sunset had faded, glowing coals were ready for cooking.

"What's the menu tonight?"

"Bush hash. Fry potatoes, onions, and Spam in a little oil and you've got it made, pardner!"

"Sounds good. Anything I can do?"

"You can start dicing."

After enjoying dinner, Jeff regained the comfort of his sleeping bag. Lying on his back and lulled by the fire, he gazed into the sky. *It always amazed him how many stars were visible away from the brightness and pollution of cities. Up on the mountain, there seemed more points of light than darkness.* Jeff remained respectfully silent. It was hard to comprehend the distance of stars; *some he was viewing had burnt out **millions of years ago**, yet their light, traveling 186,000 miles per second, was just now reaching earth!*

Jeff was interrupted by a spectacular occurrence: the fiery trails of two shooting stars crossed one another and disappeared in the night. Astonished, he called to his grandfather and excitedly described the once-in-a-lifetime event. Gramps offered his congratulations, then explained what he knew about this heavenly phenomenon. One interesting fact: *most shooting stars were smaller than silver dollars.*

Jeff's grandfather settled before the fire and retrieved a harmonica from his shirt pocket; soon he was mouthing a pleasing melody of quavering notes.

Jeff was impressed by the tonal range of this simplistic instrument— *such a variety of sounds and styles.* He tried harmonizing with Gramps's improvised tune; *it was a good thing enjoyment didn't depend upon proficiency!*

A strange *"hoohoooooing"* came drifting across the lake.

"What was THAT?"

"That, my friend, is a black bear calling for a companion."

"You're kidding! Sounds like an owl, doesn't it?"

Gramps cupped his hands and with a low guttural voice, tried to imitate the strange call. Then he beckoned Jeff.

"You try."

"HOO HOOOO," the boy called, then waited. Soon, he was thrilled by a distant answer. To make sure it wasn't coincidence, he called again. *Sure enough, there came another response!*

For several entertaining minutes, Jeff and the bear "conversed." After their calling finally subsided, Gramps applauded his grandson on the success of his mimicry.

It was bedtime. Walking over, Gramps wrapped his sinewy arms around his grandson and gave him an affectionate hug.

"See you in the morning, buddy. Sleep well and pleasant dreams!"

CHAPTER 15

DAY 5:

THE FIRE TOWER;
LEAVING THE MOUNTAIN

The next morning, Jeff awoke to a hot fire and sizzling bacon. Springing out of his sleeping bag, he dressed and joined his grandfather sipping cocoa.

Gramps handed Jeff a bowl of oatmeal garnished with nuts, raisins, and syrup.

"Roughing it again, are we?" the boy joked as he downed spoonsful of the tasty concoction.

A sizable Canadian jay landed in a nearby tree. As Gramps was cutting a slice of bacon from the rind, the jay descended, grabbed hold, and began a tug-o-war with Gramps. Jeff had never seen a wild bird behave so boldly as this one, obviously no newcomer to such piracy.

After allowing a brief stalemate, Gramps eased his grasp and chuckled as the jay flew off with its prize. Minutes later, it returned with a raucous cry.

"Not YOU again!"

Recognizing this "give-an-inch/take-a-mile" psychology, Gramps cut off a barely liftable chunk, which seemed to satisfy the voracious bird.

After breakfast, the campers policed the grounds. Revitalized by rest, food, and fine weather, they shouldered their packs and headed for the summit.

Compared with yesterday's ordeal, the remaining hour's ascent was an enjoyable challenge. They negotiated a steep and lengthy rise, then waded through a plateau of wildflowers and windblown grasses. After surmounting a mazelike jumble of weathered boulders, they breathlessly scrambled up the wind-scoured dome capping Lookout Mountain.

Jeff hooted with delight. "WE MADE IT!"

A fire tower dominated his view. Crisscrossed metal girders rose to dizzying heights, supporting a lookout station.

Jeff turned to Gramps.

"Want to climb it?"

"No thanks, son. There was a time I'd go for such daredevilry, but no more. You go ahead."

The boy inspected the fire tower. Though its steel frame was firmly affixed in bedrock with concrete and guy wires, passing clouds made the structure appear to sway. Shaking off this optical illusion, Jeff grasped the first rung of the narrow ladder.

"Well, here goes."

Gramps squinted upward to follow his grandson's progress; at about eighty feet, Jeff stopped. The elder man figured the moving clouds and unfamiliar height were beginning to erode his grandson's confidence. Indeed, indecision had crept into Jeff's thoughts as his hands grew clammy and his stomach queasy. These sensations intensified when he peered down at the diminutive form of his grandfather.

Gramps cupped his hands and shouted upward. "Think you've gone high enough? Do you want to come down?"

His grandfather's words provided incentive the boy needed. "*It's all in your mind*" Jeff repeated as he concentrated on looking up. He didn't want to back down now; he had made it this far and was determined to overcome his apprehension. He resumed pulling his body upward, conquering one rung at a time. Although he did not question the ladder's steel welds, he felt better dividing his weight equally between two rungs.

Now he was about twenty feet from the cubicle's hatch door. He was beginning to feel better. *COME ON, KEEP GOING!* Another rung. *Making this climb was like negotiating life itself: Big things could be accomplished one small step at a time.*

He was almost there; just ten feet remained. Jeff picked up the pace... *Finally, he had made it!*

Taking one hand off the ladder, he opened the trap door and squeezed through its narrow opening. Feeling a rush of relief, he sat panting on the floor of the confined space. After catching his breath, he stood up and peered through the surrounding glass panels.

WHAT A VIEW! Crystal Creek was a silver ribbon meandering through miniature trees; beneath granite mountains, the Ausable lakes gleamed. *It felt wonderful to be so high—like being in a tree fort atop the world!*

A sudden rush of wind rattled the tower. On the horizon, great thunderheads billowed; their upper cotton-like formations seemed to breathe as they grew in size above a bottom layer of dense gray. As they approached, the sky turned dark. Suddenly, a staccato barrage of ice pellets rattled the hut.

Jeff had learned hail was formed when updrafts drove rain to subfreezing altitudes. The frozen pellets eventually fell, taking on new moisture. Each time the wind returned the hail to its former heights, a frozen layer was added—a cycle repeated until the hailstones grew too heavy. *Imagine the turbulence required to support record hailstones the size of softballs!*

As suddenly as the hailstorm arrived, it passed. Jeff followed the ever-changing cloud mass as it moved relentlessly toward Tree Top Lodge. The rumbling of distant thunder announced the coming of a more common phenomenon—thundershowers. Jeff loved thunderstorms, when the sky became a spectacular battleground illuminated by crackling bolts of supercharged electricity.

He knew lightning, given the right precautions, could be enjoyed rather than feared. Being in a house or car while avoiding water, tall trees, high ground, and conductive metal would permit the safe enjoyment of this spectacle. The high metal tower, a prime conductor, was rendered safe by a lightning rod. If lightning struck, Jeff knew its electricity would be channeled down the attached copper cable and diffused harmlessly into the ground.

Thunder, he had learned, was caused by the explosive expansion of air superheated by lightning. The bigger and hotter the lightning bolt, the

94

louder and longer the accompanying thunder. By multiplying the speed of sound by the number of seconds it took thunder to follow the lightning flash, the distance and progress of any storm could be approximated.

Within fifteen minutes, the showers ended. While waiting for the tower ladder to dry, Jeff imagined himself a forest ranger surveying the countryside for fires. Each year, rangers' vigilance saved thousands of acres of timber; *spotting one fire might compensate for countless hours spent in this isolated cubicle.*

Jeff had learned that fires could be beneficial, even essential, to forests. They return nutrients to the soil and clear diseased trees and choking undergrowth, making room for vigorous new growth. One species of pine actually relies on fire in its reproductive cycle: only extreme heat causes its cones to forcibly open and scatter seeds about the forest floor.

Jeff felt ready to descend. Backing down through the opened hatch, he grasped the first rung. He paused to adjust to the unsettling altitude before making a smooth descent.

———————— · ————————

"Welcome to earth, Jeffrey! How'd you like it up there? Make friends with any eagles?"

Jeff grinned. "How about that hail and now bright sunshine!"

Gramps nodded. "Want to eat?"

They unwrapped peanut butter and jelly sandwiches, which they consumed with fruit and iced tea. Following lunch, Jeff undressed to his briefs and dozed the remainder of the afternoon.

Jeff was awakened by the cool shadow of a passing cloud. Gramps approached.

"It's two-thirty. We'd better be starting back."

Their descent of the mountain held further adventures. Certain sections offered running leaps off numerous ledges; jumping and landing onto successively lower levels, Jeff would run a few steps and again take to the air.

Such sport demanded concentration and surefootedness. With youthful abandon, Jeff whooped and bounded his way down the mountain. He recalled "Powder Pete" Pelletier, a skiing buddy who was the best ledge jumper he had ever seen. Though Jeff couldn't match Pete's "go-for-it" pace, he was making good time and enjoying himself. From time to time, he'd pause and allow his grandfather to catch up. Then, playing Tortoise and Hare, he would shoot ahead down the mountainside.

Finally, they reached their canoe.

CHAPTER 16

RETURN TO TREE TOP LODGE

As the hikers boarded their canoe, they turned in the direction of an increasingly shrill whine. Out from the horizon, tiny specks soon became three jet fighters. Splitting the air with a high screaming whistle, they banked in tight "V" formation just above the treetops and disappeared in a roll of diminishing thunder.

"Wow! Where'd THEY come from?"

"Allison Air Base, about a hundred miles north of here."

"How fast do they fly?"

"Their top speed's around 1,200 miles per hour—faster than the speed of sound."

Jeff wondered how early Native Americans might have reacted seeing these gleaming Thunderbirds—*strange, silver Gods that disappeared as quickly and mysteriously as they arrived.*

The return paddle proved uneventful. After casting thirty minutes at Tall Pines and Snag Pool, they lay down their tackle and stroked home.

Arriving at Tree Top Lodge, the famished duo was greeted by Ma Forster. Hugs were exchanged and adventures reviewed. Promising more details, the returnees washed, changed, and bee-lined for the dining room. There, they hungrily surveyed the spread: roast venison, wild rice, sweet potatoes, artichokes, and more cider.

"Grandma, you outdid yourself again!"

"What are you boys waiting for?" Grandma grinned as eager hands moved from one steaming mound to another. "Save room for dessert," she called out above sounds of forks scraping plates.

When dinner and conversation were done, Jeff rose slowly and patted his swollen belly.

"No midnight munchies tonight, for sure!" he groaned contentedly. "Thanks for the great meal, Grandma."

"You're welcome, Jeffrey."

After helping with dishes, Jeff followed the enclosed walkway up to the main lodge. He entered the living room and ensconced himself on the living room couch before the great hearth. As he was being lulled by its hypnotic blaze, he felt Gramps's firm grip on his shoulders.

"Want to hear a ghost story before bed?"

"How about a rain check?" Jeff was too relaxed and tired to best appreciate one of Gramps's noted thrillers. Although fictitious, most tales raised goose bumps before invariable shudders at their chilling conclusions.

"But I'd sure appreciate one of your great rubs" he added hopefully.

"Compliments will get you everywhere!" Gramps smiled as his strong hands kneaded the kinks in Jeff's shoulders.

It was amazing how rejuvenated sore muscles felt after even a brief massage.

Most amazing was the vital need of physical touch to most animals, including humans. Though fed, sheltered, and "handled," orphaned animals often died; seemingly, the unique touch of their own species was required for their survival.

Before retiring, Jeff posed the inevitable question.

"Are we trying for the trout tomorrow?"

"Let's first run the rapids draining the Upper Lake. If the weather's still good, we might hike to Shanty Brook for a picnic; afterward, we can head upriver and give our friend another try. What do you say?"

"Excellent! When do we start?"

"I'll leave that up to you. You can sleep in a bit, if you'd like."

—————— · ——————

The next morning, Jeff arose leisurely at 9 o'clock. He shared a hearty breakfast with his grandparents, then began packing his gear. Jeff noticed his camera. An avid photographer, he had been so involved this trip he hadn't taken a single picture. Seeing his grandparents together offered a good opportunity to take a candid photo. Adopting an effective strategy, Jeff focused on an inconspicuous spot equidistant from his unsuspecting subjects. At the opportune moment, he swung and aimed his camera at his laughing grandparents. He quickly shot several pictures, knowing the follow-ups often produced the best candids. *Enlarged and framed, one would make a nice surprise gift.*

It was time to go.

"Where are we meeting you, Grandma?"

"At the boathouse."

"What if we're late?"

"I'll have my knitting or a book with me."

Gramps winked at his grandson.

"Your grandmother always likes being prepared."

Jeff thanked Ma Forster for breakfast, then hugged and kissed her goodbye. Packing his camera and hefting an armload of supplies, he headed downstairs to the dock path.

CHAPTER 17

RIDING THE RAPIDS;

A PICNIC AT SHANTY BROOK

When Jeff arrived at lakeside, he picked up a flat, circular pebble. Cocking and snapping his elbow and wrist, he forcefully flung it onto the calm lake. The pebble skipped eight times, creating a line of expanding concentric rings. *Eight was good; his record, an impressive thirteen.*

They boarded the canoe. During the paddle to lake's end, Gramps briefed his grandson on rapids-running.

"Learn to react to two words: 'pull' and 'cross-pull.' On 'pull,' strongly draw your paddle toward you, using quick, shallow strokes. On 'cross-pull,' do the same, but on the other side of the bow."

Gramps further cautioned, "Keep in mind, the stream is deceptively powerful. If you go overboard, keep your cool and don't fight the current. Lie on your back with your head raised and your legs extended, and let the current carry you feet-first downstream. Wait until you hit a slow eddy, then swim to safety.

"Now, run all this back to me so I'll know you've got it. In a stressful situation, you sometimes don't have time to think."

Jeff repeated Gramps's instructions until they heard the sound of rapids approaching lake's end. The droning murmur grew more pronounced until, at the boathouse, the noise had amplified to a low reverberating roar. They left the canoe and hiked downstream for a better look.

"Boy, this stretch doesn't give you a chance for warm-up, does it?" Jeff commented, surveying the turbulence. "What route should we take?"

Stepping to the water's edge, Gramps pointed midstream.

"See that dark 'V' slick? We'll aim for its center and paddle hard. Hopefully, we'll shoot through with enough momentum to angle us over and past those two big hydraulics rooster-tailing at midstream. From there, we follow the main current back to the left."

Gramps pointed to a cross-stream line of white water seething over a shallow rock ledge.

"If we get by that, we're home free to roller coaster a fun series of remaining hydraulics."

"Gramps, what are hydraulics?"

"Hydraulics," his grandfather explained, "are places where the current sweeps over underwater obstructions, causing depressed pockets of water followed by ascending waves. Some rivers have hydraulics so big they can swallow a twelve-man raft!"

Though the ones Jeff viewed did not approach such magnitude, he could see why they were bypassed by most.

The two memorized their course before returning to the canoe.

"Here, you'll want your helmet."

After ensuring Jeff's was snugly cinched, Gramps made a final check.

"Life jacket secure?"

"Yes, Sir!"

"OK...we're OFF!"

Pushing into the calm water, they pointed their bow toward the white turbulence seething below lake's end. Jeff's senses throbbed, his stomach tightened. On Gramps's orders, they increased their speed.

"R e a d y?...HERE WE GO-O-OOOO!"

The canoe pitched and slid down the first dark slick into a wall of surging foam. Rushing up to its drenching crest, they burst through to be swept down into a maelstrom of thundering water. They felt almost weightless while tossed like a toy boat up and down steep inclines of foaming white.

"Boulder ahead! Pull, pull, pull!"

Only quick reflexes and desperate levering prevented collision as they scraped alongside the menacing mass. With momentum gone, they were at the mercy of an inexorable current driving them off course.

"Pull, pull…cross-pull!"

Jeff could barely hear his grandfather's commands above the din of the raging torrent. He stabbed his paddle back into the foam and levered the bow away from a fast-approaching boulder. ANOTHER CLOSE CALL! Barely recovered, they resumed paddling in time to squeeze between two boulders and brush by a third.

Now they found themselves caught in a tremendous crosscurrent that swept them down and sideways into a furious boil of water. Dead ahead and fast approaching loomed jagged, unyielding stone. With a superhuman effort, Gramps bore down mightily on his flexed paddle… "*SNAP*"!

The sickening sound announced the seriousness of their predicament. With only one paddle, they were now at the current's mercy. By the time Gramps had retrieved the spare paddle, it was too late. Jeff felt a momentary helplessness, then a strange, inexplicable feeling of calm.

"Hold o-o-nnnnn!…" Gramps screamed. "Aaaaaaaaagh!"

With a jarring crunch, they slammed into knife-edge stone.

The canoe made a terrible grating sound as tons of water pressure caused it to bend, then tip.

Jeff yelled, then held his breath as the impact threw him overboard. Vanishing beneath the undertow, he was carried some thirty feet downstream before surfacing and gasping for air. Gramps watched helplessly as water again surged over his grandson. Jeff tried timing his breathing with the rise and fall of the waves, remembering to extend his arms and float feet first with legs flexed to protect his head from injury. After being swept a hundred yards farther downstream, Jeff swam for the eddy of a huge boulder. Finally, he dragged himself onto the shore and momentarily collapsed. He raised his head long enough to see his half-immersed grandfather still stranded and clinging to the teetering wreckage ever threatening to dislodge and be swept downstream.

Jeff was exhausted mentally and physically, yet a surge of adrenalin enabled him to stumble upstream to where his grandfather clung.

Gramps called weakly, "Lad, the guide rope…catch it!"

He coiled the rope and hurled it toward shore, but it fell short. He retrieved it and tried again. *Another miss!* After a half-dozen unsuccessful attempts, Gramps was forced to rest. He tried again. This time, the line landed on a rock.

"Grab a stick and see if you can hook the rope," Gramps shouted.

Jeff returned with a branch. After several attempts, he snagged the line. Suspense mounted as he gingerly inched it toward himself… "Got it!"

"Good boy! Now pull it taut and tie your end to a heavy rock. I'll shove the canoe off and hold on."

When all was ready, Gramps pushed off the boulder and clung tightly.

As predicted, the tethered craft swung around like the sweeping hand of a clock. When it reached the shallows, Gramps staggered ashore.

Jeff hurried over and gave his grandfather a relieved hug.

"You OK?"

"Give me time and I'll think about it." Gramps paused. "Shaky, if you want to know the truth!"

"Me, too!" Jeff shook his head in relief. "WHEW!"

Both were thankful they had survived the crisis with only frayed nerves and slight bruises.

Gramps announced, "Leave the canoe. I'll come back for it later."

On the hike back to the upper boathouse, Jeff thought about the accident. *It was interesting how calm and clear-thinking he had remained during the crisis*; his relative relaxation had reduced the chance of injury. Would he shoot the rapids again? *Most likely, but not today!* Jeff realized there was an element of danger in much that we do, but now he knew firsthand the value of preparation and knowledge in coping with any emergency.

When they arrived at the boathouse, Ma Forster was there to greet them.

"What happened to you two...you look like drowned dishrags! Took a spill, eh?"

"Of sorts." Gramps feigned casualness, not wishing to overly upset his wife. Since he hadn't elaborated, she let the subject drop, knowing she would get the details later.

"Bet you're ready to eat!"

"You can say that again!"

"I've got a nice lunch waiting at Shanty Brook. Hold on for fifteen minutes and we'll picnic there."

They chorused their approval.

In the boathouse, Gramps and Jeff changed into their spare clothes. The three then hoisted their supplies and set out for Shanty Brook. Jeff led the way, stalking Indian-like along the leaf-littered path. A mile inland, within a scenic grove of beech and maple, he stopped. Signaling for silence, he tried to locate the source of a drumming sound echoing through the woods.

A ruffed grouse stood atop a fallen log, its foot-high body upraised with banded tail fanned like a turkey's. Beating short, stiff wings against air close to its body, it produced a loud booming noise attempting to attract a mate.

While enjoying the rare concert, Jeff admired the handsome bird's brown and black plumage perfectly camouflaged with its surroundings. When Jeff moved his head, the bird exploded off in zig-zag flight through the trees. *Such escape tactics must surely challenge the sharpest-eyed marksmen!*

Soon the hikers entered a sunlit clearing overlooking a boulder-strewn ravine. Musically cascading down the mountainside, Shanty Brook spilled off numerous waterfalls into clear, terraced, pools.

What an idyllic place! Jeff's skin tingled in the refreshing breeze. Shedding his sneakers, he bounded barefoot across sun-warmed shelves of stone smoothed by centuries of water-washed gravel.

While Ma Forster unpacked lunch, her grandson jumped from boulder to boulder, eagerly exploring each pool. Clamoring up past picturesque waterfalls and foamy chutes, he discovered new pools above.

Jeff peered into the bubbling, transparent depths of one small, deep cauldron. He spied several jewel-like trout weaving in the current. Though varied lures were tried, only a wriggling worm enticed them. One eager youngster gulped the hook too deeply; after delivering a merciful stroke with his pen knife, Jeff left the dead fish as a stream-side treat for some scavenger.

Perhaps this raccoon will find it, he thought upon discovering tell-tale prints in soft sediment.

For a science project, he had surrounded similar tracks with a cardboard frame and filled it with plaster of Paris. The dried mold contained a perfect imprint of the animal spoor.

Many fossils were similarly formed: silt covering an organism hardened into rock; after the plant or animal decomposed, its fossil imprint remained.

"Lunch time!" Ma Forster called.

Jeff scrambled over boulders and down ledges to arrive breathless.

The menu was simple but good: hard-boiled eggs, ham and cheese sandwiches topped with Durkee's dressing, and washed down with iced tea. A candy bar completed the meal.

Inspired by his surroundings, Jeff sat down after lunch and composed a poem:

Grip of Winter, newly gone
Sunshine's warmth turns birds to song
Upon the Earth all trees make friends
Continue so till summer's end.
Unfolding nature, first morning dew,
Emerging butterflies of brilliant hue,
Woods and meadow's varied song,
Life's true cycles, never wrong.

He read it to his appreciative grandparents, then bid them goodbye and headed downstream. After a short hike, he arrived at *The Chute*. Here, the stream squeezed between opposite cliffs and sped down a steep, mossy incline.

What fun it was in summer, sliding down the slippery slope and being swept downstream in a Jacuzzi-like rush of bursting air bubbles!

The fifty-yard "ride" would be repeated until swimmers felt like proceeding downstream to *The Diving Rock*. At this deep-water bend, divers could climb and leap off granite shelves four, eight, fifteen, and twenty feet high. The particularly adventurous would climb a birch tree growing at the cliff's brink; edging out onto one springy branch, daredevil divers would plunge thirty feet. The dive was all the more hair-raising because the stream below was just ten feet deep, necessitating an accurate belly-smacking entry.

The lower heights suited Jeff just fine.

Exploring the silent underwater world was another pleasurable pastime. Donning facemask, snorkel, and flippers, he would mingle with minnows tolerant of his slow-moving presence. The resident school created impressive light shows, ever-turning and flashing in bright, mysterious unison.

A puff of silt might reveal a crayfish defensively gesturing with outstretched claws. When approached, it would *snap* its fanned tail and dart backward to the underlying protection of a nearby stone. *Catching crayfish was always fun.*

What a day—the rapids, grouse, fishing, picnicking, and exploring! Satiated and fatigued, Jeff trekked downstream to join his grandparents. Before bedtime, he and Gramps planned a final search for King.

CHAPTER 18

DAY 6:

MORE FISHING

The sixth day brought continued fine weather: warm and still, with an occasional breeze wrinkling the water. Soon after Jeff descended the porch steps, he began yelling.

"Gramps, Gramps! Quick…come quick!"

Jeff's grandfather hurried to the porch railing and called down.

"What on earth have you got hold of?"

His grandson was engaged in a "tug-of-war" with a six-foot black snake, half of which was firmly lodged within its earthen hole. The boy knew this reptile was a nonpoisonous constrictor that suffocated its prey with ever-tightening loops of its muscular body.

The snake was surprisingly strong for its size; swelling its scales tightly against the hole, it defied extraction. After a lengthy stalemate, the boy reluctantly eased his grasp and watched the snake's tail slither from view.

Jeff was flushed with excitement.

"Did you *see* it, Gramps?"

"That I did!" Gramps exclaimed, adding "your 'friend' likes hunting about the cabin; it and a local owl are the two best mouse catchers around."

Jeff picked up a smooth, translucent membrane lying nearby. It was the snake's skin, shed to allow room for new growth.

"When a snake outgrows its old skin, it rubs its head against wood or stone; after snagging some skin, the snake slithers out of its old covering."

Jeff decided to save the peeled replica of its owner for biology class.

It was time to head back to Snag Pool. Reality gnawed as Jeff thought about the big brook trout. *This was his next to last day.* Feeling a wave of urgency, he realized how badly he wanted this fish.

Could the trout have left Snag Pool? If need be, Jeff would search elsewhere.

He and Gramps inspected the bait trap. Finding several plump shiners, they transferred them to their bait container and set off.

A white seagull passed overhead. Jeff inquired why this sea bird was so far inland. Gramps explained that gulls are well-adapted for long flight and can thrive on varied diets in differing habitats.

Two sleek doe grazed on trailside bushes. As the humans approached, the deer froze and stood erect, their large, upraised ears sensing the slightest sound while their wet noses detected the strong downwind scent of the intruders. True to the name "white-tail," their long bushy tails shot up like white warning flags. With graceful, stiff-legged bounds, they disappeared easily into the undergrowth.

Upon arriving at Snag Pool, Jeff rigged a live minnow.

"OK, fella, do your stuff!" he cajoled as he tossed his bait. Soon he felt it darting and tugging. If the trout was below, it would be alerted to such sporadic activity. However, fifteen minutes and several locations later, the untouched minnow was returned to the bait bucket.

In the glassy flow above Snag Pool, both fishermen tried again. But, time after time, they reeled in lures attached to nothing but an occasional tuft of aquatic weed.

At Tall Pines Pool, they experienced the same results. Ultimately, their outing ended with a subdued paddle home that, due to their lowered morale, seemed longer and more tiring than usual. Nursing his mental wounds, Jeff realized: *Just one more day!*

CHAPTER 19

DAY 7:

THE LAST DAY

On the last morning of Jeff's vacation, his grandfather had to assist Ranger McCabe with unexpected business. Gramps approached his grandson.

"Sorry I have to bow out again, son. But you enjoyed soloing last Monday, so you'll be OK again, right?"

Jeff nodded. Intent on enjoying his newfound freedom, he hugged his grandfather goodbye before descending to the lake.

Arriving at the dock, he raised the bait bucket and discovered some nocturnal marauder had feasted on the meal within. Replacement bait was needed before the trout finished its morning feeding. Jeff did not anticipate a problem: crickets and grasshoppers abounded in the upstream meadows.

Almost mechanically, he stroked past Snag Pool and the glassy shallows to beach below the fast water draining Tall Pines Pool. While making his way upstream, Jeff decided to fish in reverse order.

THE MONARCH OF TALL PINES POOL

Tall Pines Pool...it was a place he would never forget! The ancient hemlocks, mossy stones, and shining water were a soothing balm. *Back home, whenever he might desire a "breather," he need only recall standing atop these granite heights listening to the trees and falling water.*

Jeff cast to center pool and watched the flashing spinner bump along the bottom. Once again, he reeled in his untouched offering. He continued casting to the pool's holding areas, disappointment mounting as a nagging sameness persisted: *still no fish!*

He gazed with perplexed sadness over the beautiful pool and thought about having to leave it for the last time. *Whatever the day's outcome, he would treasure the exciting events of the past week.*

Before leaving, Jeff recalled Gramps's advice to fish potentially productive water missed by most anglers. The only place not yet tried was the seething turbulence beneath the falls.

Jeff hesitated, then shrugged. *Why not? A quick cast would complete coverage of the pool.*

He side-armed a half-hearted cast out toward the falls. *Chink!* The lure hit a bordering rock, dropped into the froth, and was sucked below in the undertow. In an instant, it was snagged.

"Darn!" *To lose a good lure on an unnecessary cast—this was a last inconvenience he didn't need! He'd pull again. If the lure didn't come free, he'd break it off and move on.*

Steadily, Jeff drew back until the line neared its breaking point. It was then he felt a tremor telegraphing up through the line.

Wide-eyed, Jeff listened incredulously to his now clicking reel. *Strange! His moving line was heading not downstream, but up! Maybe he had snagged driftwood being carried upstream by a back eddy.*

When his line was drawn *beneath* the pouring water, Jeff leaned forward. *Things were getting very interesting...*

A powerful tug nearly tore the rod from Jeff; tightening his grip, he reared back to feel a big body moving in the current.

IT'S THE TROUT...THE TROUT...

I'VE JUST HOOKED THE TROUT!... "Yaaa-HOOooooo!"

116

Jeff struck twice, further setting the hook. He feared the trout might set off on a rush that neither nerves nor tackle could withstand. Yet, the quarry swam with such apparent lack of concern that Jeff questioned whether it was aware or even cared that it was hooked. For a time it remained out of sight, playing a non-yielding tug-of-war with the relatively insignificant pressure being exerted against its wolf-like head. Still, King's sheer size caused the rod to groan in an ever-tightening arc.

While the fish casually traversed the open depths, Jeff cautiously held on. When the line continued moving, Jeff tightened the reel's drag, to no avail.

Will NOTHING stop him? He watched his lengthening line again angle beneath the falls. *How could this happen?*

Centuries of backwashed current must have eroded an underwater cavern underlying the granite overhang. Harbored within this shaded recess, breathing oxygenated water, the fish was protected from predators. *No wonder it had eluded capture for so long!*

So...the mystery was solved, but the struggle was not, as another hard jerk nearly wrenched the rod from Jeff. Yet, after the boy recovered, the creature resumed its stubborn refusal to be coaxed from the falls. It was just as well; in these early stages, Jeff was happy to play it cautiously for fear that heavy-handed tactics against so fresh and strong a fish would be inviting trouble. If pressure were maintained, he reasoned, the trout would eventually tire.

After several minutes, the lad tried cranking the big trout to the surface. Slowly, he drew back as much as he dared. The fish didn't budge. The boy gritted his teeth. *HARD...HARDER...HA-ARRR-DER still. This was obviously more than he had planned for!*

Again, he reared back until he felt he should pull no more. With his rod bowed in a full power arc, he felt attached to an immovable snag. Jeff tried a pumping method used in battling big game fish: pulling back his rod, then quickly dropping the tip while reeling in the slack. He repeated the process, yet every time line was regained, the fish would click off an equal amount—creating a frustrating stalemate.

Should he tighten the drag? No. Further adjustment might cause the line to break.

Jeff drew the contorted rod back until he yielded in an exasperated cry of admiration and disbelief.

One…more…Tiimmmme! Fearing for his tackle, he eased off yet again.

Some fish, you! The boy was beginning to marvel at King's determination. The uncompromising sameness of the drama was beginning to wear. *How long could he hold out against this opponent?* The struggle had developed into a battle of nerves.

Now Jeff plucked and twanged the line. Though this strategy was often effective on sulking fish, it failed to annoy King into moving. Almost purposefully, the fish refused to show that it even acknowledged the fisherman's presence. The boy wiped his brow as he contrasted the trout's lethargic tactics to its former spirited battle with Gramps. *Something was bound to happen—HAD to happen!*

Whether it was the tapping, the pulling, or simply the creature's desire for change, something finally appeared to be working.

He's starting to move…He's coming out!

Jeff reeled in slack as the fish glided out into center pool. The angler traced the moving line, searching intently. A patch of foam drifted aside… *THERE!*

Near bottom, King's dark length undulated.

Jeff heart began pounding as the trout, for the first time, allowed itself to be drawn upward. Growing more visible, it ascended until its mossy back broke surface. Now it casually finned atop the gurgling current.

Jeff swallowed in disbelief. King would have looked large anywhere, but in this small pool, its size seemed magnified. It was BIG—*bigger than he ever imagined!*

King's vermiculated back gleamed above broad flanks aflame with crimson spots haloed in blue.

The trout began shaking its head and chomping on the spinner protruding from its toothy jaw. Purposefully, it dove and rubbed its head among bottom stones to rid itself of the tenacious steel. Foiled, it shot for the surface, shaking and arching its shining body before disappearing into the froth.

"Whew-whee, what a Fish!" Jeff yelled to the breeze.

Taut line hissed as the trout zigzagged about the pool. With its surges keeping Jeff on the defensive, he couldn't tell how well his hook and line were holding. One thing he knew: *the fish was still on!*

As King raced about, its bright colors flashed up through the crystalline depths. Only minutes had elapsed, yet the excitement and suspense of the struggle seemed to stop time. Against such light tackle, the fish would remain in control until tired. Meanwhile, it had one thought on its mind: ESCAPE.

Now the humming line cut through water and accelerated as its angle flattened.

HERE HE COMES!

In a heart-stopping leap, King surged into sunlight, framed by far-flung droplets. One, two, three times, Jeff was mesmerized by his opponent's leaps. After a resounding slap and quick flip, the fish bore below, only to regain momentum for yet another midair assault. Like a sailfish, it tail-walked several yards backward before landing on the semi-taut line. Jeff barely reacted in time; by lowering and thrusting his rod forward, he had created enough slack to withstand the trout's falling weight.

Continuing to battle, King dove for the bottom, pumping Jeff's rod downward. Then, up and out, his desperate surges carried him high into the spray-filled air. Such frenzied leaps would have winded most, but this fish seemed impossible to conquer.

"Please stay on! PLEASE!" Jeff gripped the rod and hung on.

Meanwhile, the wily beast tried yet another tactic: it twisted and rolled itself up in the line. Once it somehow freed itself from this constraint, King became seemingly enraged. Off it shot like a bone fish, spray rooster-tailing behind speeding line as it streaked into the fast water below. Now there was no stopping him as Jeff stood with hands overhead thrilling to the tune of the whirring reel

ZZZZZZZZZZZZZZZZZZZZZZZZZZZZZZZZZZZZZ

Fifty yards of line gone.

ZZZZZZZZZZZZZZZZZZZZZZZZZZZZZZZZZZZZZ

One hundred yards!

Still the fish lunged on. *Could this brute be stopped?...Could it be slowed?*

Stretched line scraped stone; metal gleamed on the near-empty spool; *still* the drag whirred its high-pitched tune. Something had to be done—*IT WAS NOW OR NEVER!* Forcing legs into motion while holding rod high, Jeff pursued the finned torpedo downstream. Tripping here, off balance there, he circumvented boulders and fallen timbers. Now, the reel whined in torment—its constant whirring an ominous reminder that little line remained. Still, the boy struggled on.

Suddenly, the rod straightened.

OH, NO! Jeff frantically reeled up slack. *Had the fish broken off?*

Suspense mounted. Then the line tightened. The trout, still on, had ended its stupendous run and was resting behind some boulder. But Jeff's relief was short-lived when the line slackened again.

120

What NOW? He reeled in more yards of limp line. While fearing the worst, he sighted a passing flash. King, trailing loose line, was heading upstream for Tall Pines Pool.

It was his opponent's first major error: Not even this fighter could long withstand the opposing forces of rod *and* current. *Now if only hook and line would hold!*

CHAPTER 21

THE BATTLE ENDS

King fought his way up-current, straining to reach Tall Pines Pool. By the time Jeff had recovered all slack, the trout was swimming over the pool's brink.

HE'S HEADING FOR THE FALLS!

In a desperate attempt to arrest its relentless charge, Jeff reared back. For thirty minutes, such efforts had gone unrewarded; now, the reel was laboring. *Cliiiiiiick—the fish was slowing! Cli-i-ick...click.*

The trout could go no further. Laboring in vain, its muscular back broke water. Now its great head was coming around. Jeff was elated.

Carried by the current, King floated slowly toward him. The fisherman managed his first smile, yet remained cautious. *Any error might still lose the prize!*

As Jeff thought this, the weary brook trout swiped its tail and ran out ten yards. However, the inexorable draw of rod and current had taken their toll; the fish lost momentum and began drifting back toward the waiting fisherman.

Several times Jeff thought the fight was over, only to have King swim maddeningly out of reach. At the end of its last spurt, it rolled and exposed its shining side. Then it righted itself, as if to keep from showing it was defeated. With the end in sight, Jeff checked his landing net. *Clearly, it was too small!*

He would try drawing the immobile trout into shallow water where he could grasp it behind its head. But King's broad girth and slimy skin would be difficult to hold. Still, there was no choice—*it HAD to be done!*

With steady tension, Jeff half-dragged his exhausted trophy until it lay at his feet. Leaning over his target, he tensed for an accurate thrust. His movement provoked another evasive flurry. Halfway across the pool, the trout lost momentum and Jeff swung it easily around. Now it drifted on its side, eye bulging, jaws opening and closing, its dorsal fin curling like a flag in final surrender. Gingerly, the fisherman drew the exhausted fish toward the shallows. There King wallowed, his bowed body swishing slowly from side to side. Flopping over, he wearily righted himself. Now, his marbled back was only inches away.

The boy drew in a slow breath, then thrust his hands down. The thrashing trout, too large for his grasp, began to slip away. Jeff threw caution aside and pounced like a cat on a mouse. Pinning his prize against the stones, he slipped his hands behind the fish's head and with a triumphant yell, hefted his trophy skyward.

WHAT A TROUT!

King's tapered bulk glistened; its beautiful flanks spotted crimson, white, and blue above a belly of deep orange.

Jeff admired his trophy, then lowered the fish and clamped a pocket scale to its lower jaw. He again lifted the trout and announced its astonishing weight: "6 pounds, 2 ounces!"

Jeff beamed and gazed about, but no one was present to witness the moment. He felt like shouting, but no other could hear. Kneeling, he placed the trout in ankle-deep water, withdrew the scale, and watched King's gills work erratically in effort to regain its breath.

He then took a length measurement: *22 inches.*

The fish lay immobile, conquered, almost docile. *It was hard believing this was the same King who minutes before had so strained line and nerve!*

Jeff basked in his accomplishment. While savoring his victory, he was faced with a most difficult decision: *What to do now?*

Of course! Mount this prize of a lifetime—hang it on a wall for all to admire.

Yet, Jeff questioned, *was that all there was to it?* Opposing thoughts had to be considered.

Above all, there was Gramps. It was he who had invited Jeff to this wonderful place and had shared the secret of this fish's existence. For the chief fishing guide of the Ausable Preserve, catching this fish would fulfill a lifetime goal.

Although no guarantee ensured Gramps ever landing this wily veteran, it seemed only fair to allow him a continuance of his quest. Jeff had thrilled in landing this fish; why shouldn't his grandfather be allowed the opportunity to enjoy the same?

The boy closed his eyes and pictured Gramps's excitement battling and capturing the fish; the image argued for the trout's preservation.

There was a second consideration: *the trout's natural bond to the pool.*

Jeff envisioned King scattering schools of minnows, bumping rocks for crayfish, and slurping floating insects. *What a contrast to the hotel trout, hanging stiff and immobile!* Although the latter was impressive, it remained an inanimate piece of stuffed skin.

By killing the magnificent fish now before him, Jeff would deprive himself and others of future quests for this honored adversary. He recounted the exciting moments leading to the Trout's capture. *These memories would never fade; why, then, should the natural beauty of King's colors?* The boy closed his eyes and re-envisioned the fish hanging on a plaque. Although the image remained impressive, he felt saddened by the thought.

Jeff had made up his mind. He would not kill this fish.

He carefully unhooked King. Though free to go, it curiously remained finning at his feet. Jeff knelt and wet his hands to prevent damaging the fish's protective slime coating. He ran his hand along the trout's side, noting its cool firmness. Repeatedly, he moved the fish forward and backward, forcing water past its gills so it could regain its breath. Still the brook trout remained, seemingly unafraid of the two-legged creature hovering overhead.

Jeff bent down and gave the trout an affectionate pat. With a reassuring push, he coasted it outward.

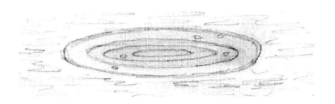

For a time, it lay finning; then it slowly sank to disappear into the depths of center pool.

CHAPTER 22

THE RETURN TO TREE TOP LODGE

By now, the thrill of victory had subsided into paradoxical feelings vacillating between joy and disappointment. The goal so sought had been realized, yet in his moment of triumph, Jeff felt an anticlimactic letdown. Emotions had peaked during the battle; their sudden release following the fish's capture left the boy physically and emotionally drained.

Jeff lingered at poolside until fatigue set in. Seeking a soft bed of grass, he lay down.

Several hours later, he awoke rejuvenated. Immediately, he was drawn to the pool's edge as if to ensure his previous experience had occurred. Staring into center pool, he vainly searched for the fish. In time, he bade the trout "farewell" and headed for the canoe.

While paddling home, Jeff thought about his grandfather. Though Gramps would certainly have been happy in Jeff's accomplishment, the boy reasoned Gramps might be *happiest* believing his ultimate prize remained uncaught.

What Gramps didn't know would never hurt him, Jeff concluded; thus, he chose to withhold the news. *In the meantime, it was going to be HARD not divulging such an irresistible secret! Yet if he, Jeff, returned to friends with nothing but a professed account of the "facts," who would believe him? But did it really matter? He himself knew—would forever know—what occurred that special day at Tall Pines Pool.*

Jeff returned to find Tree Top Lodge silhouetted by a flaming sunset. His grandparents were quick to greet him. Ma Forster hurried over and emotionally embraced her grandson.

"Where have YOU been? Jud and I were expecting you hours ago. You shouldn't have stayed out so long!"

Jeff looked sheepishly toward his grandfather, who offered a knowing wink. *He knew where his grandson had gone!*

"Probably would have done the same thing my last day." Seeing Jeff empty-handed, Gramps assumed the obvious: *the Trout was still at large.*

Ma Forster put her arm around her grandson and ushered him upstairs.

"What a relief to have you home safe!…How about supper? You must be famished."

But Jeff had no appetite. Staring out past the silhouette of the distant pine, he tried a forkful of food but found himself too distracted. Renewed feelings of ambivalence were taking hold; *how much he wanted to present King to his grandparents!* Jeff sighed. He would be back next spring; he hoped the trout would be there when he and his grandfather returned.

CHAPTER 23

NEWS FROM GRAMPS

Weeks passed, and then months. Then, in September, Jeff received a letter from his grandfather. Somehow, he sensed the news as he unfolded a front-page clipping from the *Keene Valley Courier*. A photograph showed Jud Forster standing in knee-deep water, proudly hefting "*the biggest brook trout ever caught in New York State.*"

Eyes misted as Jeff recalled his thrilling encounter with this very fish. He felt happy knowing his grandfather's dream had been fulfilled, yet sad losing a "friend" he would never again see in the wild. With mixed feelings, Jeff began reading the accompanying article. The last two sentences brought a smile to his face; slowly, he repeated them out loud:

"*After photographing himself with his trophy, Jud Forster did what few might have done: he returned the trout to its home.*"

"*When asked where he caught the monster, Mr. Forster signaled '***Silence***' with an upraised forefinger bisecting his widening grin.*"

Jeff lowered the paper.

It felt great knowing King was still free.

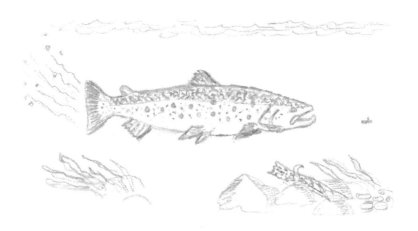

EPILOGUE

To this day, the King swims free.

——————— · ———————

Jeff never questioned his decision again.

ABOUT THE AUTHOR

Rick Crecraft grew up in a beautiful suburb of Philadelphia, Pennsylvania. As a boy, he enjoyed barefoot summers netting turtles, tadpoles, fish, snakes, and frogs from nearby ponds. These adventures, and those at Maine's Camp Kieve and Put Stowe's Adirondack Camp, provided inspiration and content for this story. Fishing the Florida Keys and reading *Sports Afield*, *Outdoor Life*, and *Field and Stream* further sparked this book's writing.

Like this Story?
Call: 610-525-1818
for
Gift Discounts

Made in the USA
Middletown, DE
14 August 2017